Deal With Toxic Family Members

7 Survival Secrets For Adult People To Set Positive Boundaries In Relationships With Parents, Siblings, And Relatives Within Five Weeks Without Cutting Ties

Written by

Lucca Zeni

mindfulpersona.com

Table Of Contents

A Free 4 Steps Guide To Understand Your Emotional Patterns is yours now!

This is a special gift for you, as you are consuming one of our books! This **4 Steps Guide** will take you through the possible patterns you have and ways to reframe them + Exercises!

Access

www.mindfulpersona.com

to get your free copy today!

Introduction

Do you frequently feel a little exhausted when a particular family member is in the same environment?

Do you fear being yourself or trying something personal because family members will take you for granted, laugh at you, or judge you?

Do you have a relative who gossips about you and criticizes your every move, trying to ruin your joy?

Perhaps your parents are extremely controlling despite being an adult and always make you feel less capable and diminished, treating you as if you were a child.

Now, if any of these instances resonate with you, keep reading to understand more about how they start.

Your Mental Health may be overwhelmed by the negativity and emotional hazards around you. Toxic family members tend to drain you emotionally with their presence. They can make your head hurt and overall sap your energy.

No doubt, every family has occasional arguments where they disagree and agree with each other later. However, if your family makes you feel worse whenever you are with them, and you experience little relief when you are away, your family is likely treading on the toxic territory.

Some of these behaviors from your family can be draining, and your encounter with them will leave you emotionally wiped out. Spending time with them will make you feel unfulfilled, frustrated, and angry. In addition, they will want you to keep giving in to their requests without you getting anything in return. As a result, you become depleted.

To some people, family is a special, genetic, or unique bond between people. For some others, it's more than just a bond. To them, family is the only place where they feel secure and completely relaxed; it is where their "**HOME**" is.

I've had to battle with family and relatives with strong personalities for many years. I grew up in an aggressive and turbulent environment, where siblings and parents were always in conflict and disagreement with each other. Uncles and aunties also greatly influenced my self-esteem, discouraging pursuing any life perspective by *patronizing and underestimating my potential.

I have an uncle who changes my countenance and the atmosphere becomes frigid immediately after he walks into a room. He has always been mean and aggressive to everyone, and he has his ways of saying things that will make anyone start doubting themselves. So each time he came around, I always wanted to run into any other room in the house, to avoid him.

After years of living in fear and pain, I realized that my uncle tends to have toxic traits. Thankfully, I know better now, and it doesn't bother me anymore. A huge weight has finally been lifted off my shoulders after my realization.

Movies would often show us the beautiful side of having a family. They like to show us what a perfect family should look like. But what if your family is different from what you see in movies? What if the dynamic of your family is very toxic? What then do you do?

A great way of coping with a toxic family is to identify and learn how to deal with them by setting boundaries. However, this book will significantly help if you don't know how to set boundaries or aren't good at enforcing them.

No doubt, boundaries can be hard to put in place, especially since you aren't used to using them. But, if you have a hard time with this, don't feel bad or give up; there is hope. This book will prepare you to be more confident in enforcing boundaries with toxic family members.

But how do you know if a family member or your entire household is toxic?

If you are in a healthy household, you should feel encouraged to share your views, feelings, and thoughts. Conversely, in an unhealthy household, they won't care about your emotions. They will find every opportunity to bring you down. They will likely slip insults about your physical health and appearance, leaving you with self-doubt and self-loath.

Toxic family members are controlling and like dominating your choices. They will either want to limit your options or want to make all decisions for you. They will force you to do things you hate repeatedly doing.

Also, if you notice that your interaction with a particular family member ends up in a confrontation, they are probably exhibiting toxic traits. It is okay to argue, but you shouldn't be fighting with them every time you have a conversation. A toxic relationship may also involve physical harm. If there is physical harm involved, you need to immediately stay away from the family member. Don't try to manage the situation or learn how to handle the violence.

Many people are stuck in the dreaded situation of dealing with toxic family members. Even if you have ungrateful, disrespectful, unreliable, and toxic family relatives, the conflict management strategies and healthy communication skills discussed in this book will help you respond appropriately to any family drama. It will set you on the right path to keep a cordial relationship with them without turning into enemies.

You can't control or change how people act; you shouldn't waste your time doing that. But you do have control over how you act. Therefore, if you have an issue with a difficult family member, focus on what you can control; how you react and behave.

As the name suggests, this book contains *seven survival secrets* to help you handle your guilt-tripping, nit-picky, and perhaps alcoholic relatives. You will learn groundbreaking information, exercises, and tools to help you set your feet on the ground in the face of emotional challenges. You will also learn how to redirect your thoughts of your current perspective of your relative's behavior.

I can assure you that after reading this book, you will have confidence and a healthy mental state to move forward in life without the fear of being criticized, judged, or harmed by toxic relatives. You will have better ways of dealing with them respectfully and with integrity.

I've been where you are right now, and trust me: It isn't a good place to be. I am a Brazilian who grew up in an aggressive and turbulent environment, where my siblings and parents were always in conflict and disagreement with me. I had to move away from my family to the UK to find a safe place where I could understand myself and get to know myself better.

I have my whole life attached to psychological studies and trying to understand people's emotions and behaviors better. I wanted to start living life on MY TERMS and be HAPPY, so I researched and read many books on how to deal with toxic family members. I learned and applied many valuable strategies, and I could sieve through them and identify what works and what wouldn't.

I've learned how to cope with adversities in my family and earn their respect by not acting as they did. I understood that I needed to prioritize the values that make people know their boundaries and not cross them, such as showing them love and empathy when confronted, showing self-control and reasonable arguments in conversations, and safely positioning myself without the FEAR of displeasing anyone. As a result, even far from the family, I still maintain contact with everyone, even on a shallow level.

Knowing that so many people like me are having a hard time dealing with their toxic relatives, I decided to write this book and share my knowledge to help others. With my strong experience and knowledge, which I am passionate about sharing, I've written this book to help people thrive and build healthier relationships with their toxic relationships.

By the end of this exciting journey, you should have a better understanding of personality disorders and their characteristics. Knowing the patterns of personalities can also help you learn how to deal with toxic people appropriately.

Are you ready to start this exciting journey with me? I'm sure this will be one of the books you want to give a 5-star review, for how grateful you will be when you get to practice the tools given to the readers.

Let's get started!

Chapter 1: What Exactly Describes an Abusive or Toxic Person?

Like arsenic, toxic people will slowly kill you. They kill your positive spirit and play with your mind and emotions. The only cure is to let them go."

Denisse Lisseth

People will interpret the word *'toxic'* differently depending on their circumstances. In scientific terms, toxic is simply any substance that is harmful or could cause harm either independently or when combined with other substances, such as poisonous gases or chemicals. But toxic can also be used to define and characterize human behavior, especially when they behave unkindly and maliciously toward other people.

This has allowed the term *'toxic person'* to be used in defining people who are extremely selfish, controlling, needy, and who covertly or outwardly manipulate others.

■ Who Is A Toxic Person?

A toxic person is anyone whose actions or behavior are negative and upsets your life. Their actions hurt you and negatively impact your life when around them.

Here are some of the signs showing that someone is toxic towards you:

- You're always baffled by their behavior
- They're manipulative and tend to get you to do things you don't want to do
- You're never relaxed or feel comfortable when they're around
- You always feel drained, upset, and angry when you interact with them
- They never apologize for their actions
- They put you in a defensive position when they're around you

■ Reasons Why People Become Toxic

A toxic person may even seem nice to you but underneath all that front is a very pervasive person who will display certain actions that will hurt you without feeling about it. However, such behaviors may be due to underlying mental conditions such as deep-rooted childhood trauma, narcissistic personality disorder (NPD), or other personal issues, including low self-esteem.

Toxic people are likely to have dark personality traits. These traits are revealed due to their tendency to *always* put their goals, needs, and interests above others, justify their actions and validate their behaviors without shame while avoiding guilt.

Although these types of people may have reasons for becoming toxic or manifesting these toxic behaviors, it doesn't make it less harmful or impactful to the victims experiencing their toxic behavior. Being manipulated can be hurtful and confusing, and it's never enjoyable. When taken to extremes, people can lose their self-confidence because they'll feel like they're always at fault.

I've been in this kind of situation, and it was a really difficult time for me as it was causing conflicts in my life. The situation was delicate and worse because it came from a toxic family member, and I didn't know how to handle it.

Toxic people can make you feel unpleasant and cause stress for the people around them. If it's not discovered and dealt with on time, it could lead to a mental and emotional breakdown, physical pain, or even depression.

■ Recognizing Toxic Behaviors In Your Life

Although the behaviors of a toxic person may not be considered a mental disorder, there could be underlying problems that can't be ruled out that make them behave in toxic ways, including personality disorder.

Recognizing the behaviors of a toxic person is beyond just what they say or do, but how they make you feel. You can identify toxic people in your life through the signs you notice. If you can see these signs, you can easily recognize and highlight their toxicity. These signs include:

- **Always Seeking Your Attention**

If you've noticed that someone always needs something from you, whether physical items, phone calls, or constant texts, they may be toxic. If they need you to support them emotionally and even show up at your doorsteps unannounced to seek benefits from you, you're dealing with someone whose behavior could be associated with a narcissistic personality disorder.

This type of person will ask for everything from you but will probably not be supportive of you in return. Instead, they'll drain you without giving anything except to make you feel uncomfortable around them. They're mostly interested only in their own self-interest. They will rather show an increased need to showcase their impressive side to receive accolades from people and show off their greatness.

■ They are Inconsistent

Although life, in general, is filled with ups and downs, part of being human is adapting to the good and bad times. However, a toxic person behaves erratically and is never consistent. They don't keep to their promises or follow through with their commitments. They're unpredictable, and you can't tell what their next action will be. People with toxic personality traits make it difficult to be there for them with their inconsistency. One minute they seem happy, yet they're totally different the next minute.

■ They Give Constant Drama

They like being in the midst of one drama or the other always. It's not a coincidence but their own making. A toxic person enjoys and thrives in these dramas. If there's no drama, they'll create one. They amplify emotions and cause conflict so that they can be at the center of everything. Some people are afraid of not being relevant or not concerned about a healthy and stable relationship; hence they become toxic.

■ There Are No Boundaries

Do you know someone who doesn't respect your boundaries, especially if you've expressed your needs and boundaries repeatedly, but they keep feigning ignorance or directly disrespecting you? These are clear signs that the person is toxic. Healthy relationships are not built on disappointments and disrespectful behaviors; they are built based on trust, and all parties should respect boundaries. However, Toxic people can't help themselves but intrude on all fronts.

■ Selfish and Manipulative

If you feel that you're being manipulated or taken advantage of, you're probably noticing one of the signs of a toxic person. Toxic people are self-centered and love manipulating the people around them to achieve their own goals. If it means making you feel bad about yourself, bending the truth, lying, exaggerating, or blowing things out of proportion to get what they want, they'll gladly do it. They care only about what they want from you and would do whatever is needed, even if it requires you to take risks that would hurt you or hurt others to get it done.

■ When Family Are Toxic

You can experience a toxic relationship with anyone at any point in time. But things can become even more complicated when toxicity is coming from family members. Depending on the type of experiences you've had or what you're currently experiencing, the family can mean several things to you and can flood your mind with complex emotions.

These feelings and emotions are either based on positive, negative, or a mix of both, combined into memories of the things you've experienced. Your feelings could run rampant, making you distressed, especially if you've lived or are currently trapped in a toxic family situation. You might even be constantly plagued with frustration, irritation, and helplessness when you think about your family instead of being glad to meet and interact with them.

What Are The Signs Your Family Could Be Toxic?

A dysfunctional or toxic family can be tricky and difficult to identify, especially if you are close to the person. You'll find it almost impossible to identify these signs as long as you're entrenched in them. But you can use some common signs to identify toxic relatives.

○ **Always Competing with You and they Show Signs of Jealousy**

While it might seem almost impossible or even ridiculous to think about this happening, the reality is that even parents can be jealous of their kids and even stay in competition with them. For example, your dad is someone that loves being in the spotlight at all times and will not allow you to feel good about yourself when needed. You've always dreamed of becoming a great basketball player and playing basketball for a big team, but he became a front desk teller agent.

Then when you were selected as your school football team captain, with the potential of you being called to play for a bigger team and with a scholarship, instead of making plans with you and allowing you to be in the spotlight, your dad started telling you all about himself, showing you pictures of his basketball years, in a way to sabotage your moment to enlighten his. His self-flattery didn't just give you a headache; you've never felt any joy or pride when he does this since your childhood. It's not absurd or new; a father can be jealous of his 15-year-old kid, which is common in toxic families.

- ○ **They Play the Victim**

Some people can't help but guilt-trip the people around them to get the things they want. Instead of simply expressing their disappointment, they'll blame everyone else for their misfortune or feelings when things don't go their way, creating a toxic environment. When you aren't available, they will tell you, "What do you mean you're not free at the moment?" If someone refuses to talk to you for days just because you were not free to accompany them somewhere or do something when they asked, you could be dealing with someone in the toxic territory.

○ **They Tend to Overreact**

Some family members overreact about everything using statements such as "You are always self-centered!"; "You never get anything right"; "You're always destroying things". When you hear this, you find it hard to defend yourself because of the subtle manipulation involved. Fine, you broke something important when you were a kid, and they flipped. But years after becoming an adult, they still flip on you over unreasonable things and then bring the past to support their claim.

○ **They Make Unhealthy Comparisons**

Everyone is completely different and has different likes, career choices, and ambitions. But because one of your siblings, maybe your younger sister, is married with two kids and an accountant, while you're still single as an assistant, your toxic relative(s) will try to set you against each other with unhealthy comparisons which could affect you, making you feel attacked and insecure.

○ **They Are Judgmental**

We all make mistakes sometimes as humans, but a toxic person will hold onto that and make sure you don't forget it. They'll flash it across your face at every opportunity, judge you, and attack your self-esteem. They'll make you feel your mistake makes you a lesser person.

○ **They Are Always Right No Matter What**

Do you know someone that never approves of whatever you do or seem to have something to say? They never liked anyone you've dated, and it's like no one would ever be good enough for you. They always have something to say about your career, your friends, choices, and everything you do. This habit is most common among parents who think they are protective of their kids but won't stay out of their businesses even when everything is working well. They're already leaning towards toxicity without realizing it.

- ○ **They Never Respect Your Boundaries**

Just like we discussed earlier, people who never respect boundaries tend to create a toxic environment. This is because they consider their feelings and never yours. As a result, they could be impulsive around you without considering any consequences. For example, they could even barge into your home unannounced even after telling them you don't appreciate it when they do that; they keep repeating it.

- ○ **They Want Conversations To Always Center Around Them**

When you're having a conversation, and after 30-minutes, you realize that everything they've talked about is only about them and not a single question asked about how you are doing or any concern about your life, it shows they want the conversation to center around them.

People like this are usually self-centered and want everything to revolve around them. If you don't allow that to happen, they could start accusing you of not caring. They also have a way of shifting the topic of conversation or an argument from the main topic or what's important to you to something related to them. Such a relationship is usually toxic because the other person doesn't really care about you.

○ **They Bring Irrelevant Details Into a Conversation And Drain Your Energy**

Have you ever come across a family member who makes you feel drained and exhausted when interacting with them? When you're trying to sort out something important to you, they will rather talk about irrelevant things and make you feel helpless. For example, they could bring in details from an argument that happened over 3 months ago to put you in the defensive spot and manipulate things in their favor instead of dealing with the situation at hand. Interacting with a toxic person can make you feel drained and defeated because of their self-centered, needy, and dramatic personalities.

Sometimes some of the characteristics listed above will not be visible to you since a lot of emotions are involved. So, to get a clearer picture, you need to view things from an outsider's perspective.

So, how come you are in a toxic family? Let's dig deeper by starting with the past.

How Was Your Childhood?

If you experienced most of the signs that we've discussed, then you might have grown up in a toxic family environment.

Meeting unrealistic expectations and standards

Family is a group of people living or coexisting together as a single unit, and each family member performs different roles to help each other. For example, it is fine when given roles that you can handle, such as taking turns doing dishes or helping with house cleaning. You could even be asked to watch over your younger ones if you're grown enough to handle simple responsibilities, and all these are still counted as normal tasks since they won't interfere with your regular school activities/career, leisure time, and your resting time.

However, if you were asked to do most of the following, it means you grew up in a toxic family.

- Take responsibility for parenting
- Providing most care for your siblings
- Discipline the younger family members
- Handle all house chores
- Heavy chores beyond your age
- Needed to provide emotional and financial support beyond your means

Getting unkind criticism

Were you harshly criticized for little mistakes? Although as humans, we all have emotions, and we may lose our tempers sometimes. But when the remarks used on you become destructive, not focused on your behaviors to help you learn and make amends, you would begin to feel intimidated, unloved, helpless, and inferior.

Never meeting your needs

Meeting the needs of a child is beyond monetary needs. They include spending time with you doing different activities that help you bond, making time to pick you up from school and not leave you waiting for hours, taking care of normal bills to make life bearable, etc.

Although nobody is perfect, a supportive family should at least be able to take care of the following:

- Your health care and well-being
- Affection, discipline, and manners
- Ensure you have an education
- Proving you with food and clothes

Several other factors would make your family less toxic, but if you lived without getting any of the discussed points above, it indicates you lived in an unhealthy family situation.

Chapter 2: Reasons Behind Repeating Unhealthy Family Patterns

66 Family is supposed to be our safe haven. Very often, it's the place we find the deepest heartache."

 Lyanla Vansant

If you've once heard that our first relationships in life are what set the standard for our future expectations, then you've heard right. As children, we absorb everything around us like a sponge. When born, we do not know how to act in society because we are born as a blank slate, so we must learn many of our social skills from our surroundings as we grow up.

For most of us, learning begins at home with our families. The most typical approach for children to learn is observing daily life. As children progress through adolescence and into adulthood, the home environment significantly impacts their identity. A child's self-esteem, socialization, and identity are shaped by how family members interact with one another and work as a social group. Therefore, this chapter will discuss how unhealthy family patterns form and the reasons behind them.

■ "Patronizing Behavior" and How Toxic People Use It against You

I didn't understand anything other than what my parents or close relatives taught or told me when I was young. I learned to accept some unhealthy behaviors, and I had to live with them. As I grew older, I became exposed, learned more things, gained more information, and saw life from a different perspective. Some things about me and the way I reason began to make me stand out from the rest of the people I grew up with. I began to see the toxicity in how my family members handled issues and how I had grown to cope with them even though I was frustrated at everything they did.

My first instinct was to correct it, but that was impossible. My family members were so stuck in their ways that everything I did seemed alien to them. It led to many arguments and clashes, and I was finally tagged as the 'different one'. I felt like I was in a spiral of confusion because my family, who was supposed to be my foundation, was making me feel so sadly insecure.

Just like me, have you ever felt like you are the family's "different one"? Do you have the impression that you're not anything like other family members? It's most likely because you are different from them, and there's nothing wrong with it. However, when dealing with toxic people, it's crucial to remember that you can't change them; thus, it's best not to push them too much. Instead, save your energy for something less stressful.

Your parents, siblings, and grandparents may find it difficult to see life differently. This is not totally their fault. They were born in an entirely different era where there was little or no knowledge of mental health and toxicity. They only know how to react based on how they were trained. Changing the lifestyle that a person has lived for decades is like trying to crack a nutshell.

As these people watch you grow up with your flaws and fragility, they will likely treat you the same way Jesus Christ was treated in Nazareth, where he was born and worked as a humble carpenter.

Jesus wasn't given credit by the people of Nazareth because he grew up in the city like every other kid. But how do you act when in this kind of situation where your opinion is totally ignored, and you were made someone with no relevance?

Toxic people are more harmful when they are family members. Abusive family ties are harmful to our inner serenity and self-esteem. One of the worst things to do when some family members act like this is to overreact. Overreacting or being confronted constantly makes the situation worse. Loud voices erupt, and everyone feels hurt and defensive. The atmosphere becomes tense, and no one is happy; thereby, nothing is solved.

Confrontation or overreacting only makes the damage worse. Your family or the people close to you will start to treat you with patronizing behavior. This behavior will make you feel irrelevant, and your feelings will gradually diminish.

First of all, calm yourself down and understand that no one is perfect. Even if you have your flaws, be kind.

What really is patronizing behavior?

Pretending to be kind while clearly talking down to someone or treating them as if they are less intelligent is the definition of patronizing. It's when toxic people talk to or act towards you as though you're insignificant or foolish. It may appear as if they are treating you in a friendly or helpful manner, yet there are traces of superiority in their voices and their use of body language.

Many years ago, I worked with a boss who used patronizing behaviors on me. When working with her on a project, I presented a draft of what we were to do to meet our goals. She smiled and said that I was a really smart guy, and my draft was mediocre. She told me that I should know better and rejected the draft without going through it halfway. Then, after discussing it with the board of directors, she called me back and said, "I actually like the draft."

What she just did was a patronizing remark with a sneer. It sounded as if she was taken aback by the fact that I had an excellent concept or opinion. It was clear that she thought I was unimportant.

When someone constantly says their pain or experience is bigger than yours, interrupts you, makes too many corrections, demeaning comments, and belittles you by being sarcastic, affirming you don't have experience or age enough to understand something, they exhibit patronizing behaviors. Recognizing when you're crossing into patronizing behavior will help you establish more good connections and communicate more effectively with mutual respect and trust. People who grew up in an environment where patronizing behaviors were the norm are more likely to exhibit patronizing behaviors when they grow older. They see it as normal and keep repeating the same destructive patterns to their children, grandchildren, and others around them.

■ 4 Reasons Why You Repeat Emotionally Destructive Patterns

Some people find themselves in a cycle of toxic relationships no matter how hard they try. For example, it has been reported that so many children of alcoholics get married to alcoholics despite vowing never to. Children of dysfunctional families are more likely to replicate this toxicity in their households. This appears to be unreasonable on the surface. Nobody wants to replicate the habits of a toxic or dysfunctional family. Several factors influence your tendency to repeat harmful behavioral patterns. The four most important reasons are listed below.

1. You are comfortable with familiar behaviors

You keep doing what you've always done because you feel secure with them, regardless of its toxicity.

It's like an introverted child that stays with a toxic friend not because she's comfortable with the toxicity. She stays because she's used to being there and is scared of meeting new people. She knows what to expect from her toxic friend and how to cope with her friend's outbursts. Her friend's toxicity becomes normal in the long run because she's scared of change or being alone.

You repeat these habits because they feel normal to you, and you know what's coming from them, even though you know they are unhealthy and not good for you. It's difficult to change; it's always easier to stick to your old habits than learn and use new skills. This is particularly true in children from toxic homes. If you were raised in toxic circumstances, toxicity would feel safe to you, and you will cling to this form of a bond, though with anxiety.

Trauma bonds are relationships in which we reproduce the dynamics we had with our primary caregivers as children. We learned what we needed to do to obtain love, which is often self-neglect, and as a result, we continue to neglect ourselves in our other relationships to receive love. The familiarity of the pain provides a sense of security.

Our minds are drawn to what feels most comfortable and what we've felt at ease with in the past. You've likely grown accustomed to a particular pattern and feel compelled to repeat it. Even if it doesn't lead to a better future, you still do it. Breaking out from a trauma bond into a healthy relationship can be terrifying since the healthy relationship feels strange.

2. *Your Younger Self Takes Control*

We all have a child within us, a younger version of ourselves who remembers life as it was when we were younger. You had a "small one" inside who was observing and learning about your own views, the beliefs of those around you, the beliefs of the world, and the beliefs of those who cared about you. Because your mind was young and sensitive in development, you learned behavior patterns and connection dynamics that became profoundly established. As a result, you may discover that an older side of you wants to say or do something in a particular way. Still, the tiny one inside you pushes you aside and chooses impulsive actions, bad ideas, or relationship choices for you.

You might try so hard to make a difference and go against the toxic behaviors you learned as a child, but the inner child stops you. This is because there are still some beliefs and mindsets that still lie within you. It takes conscious and constant decluttering to heal and leave those subconscious mindsets behind fully.

3. *To Gain Mastery And Control*

When you've had a distressing or upsetting experience, you're left feeling puzzled. As you get older, you have an unconscious desire to "relive" the terrible experience to understand what happened and ideally achieve a sense of mastery and control. As a result, you'll unintentionally replicate relationships or put yourself in situations where you're experiencing comparable emotions and have a great desire to change the result. You do this by frantically seeking someone's praise or acceptance which will never truly give it to you, or attempting to gain a sense of power and control in a relationship dynamic.

A terrible experience with a parent as a youngster or a chaotic dating situation in the past can leave us with a never-ending recollection of something we need to address. So we attempt to recreate the experience with our new partner to fix the feeling that we didn't get to a satisfactory ending. This is why, without even recognizing it, some people choose friends, lovers, colleagues, or neighbors who treat them the same way their parents or previous toxic spouse treated them.

4. *You feel undeserving of love and respect*

Our perceptions of ourselves govern all aspects of our lives. We pick up essential beliefs from every connection and experience from childhood and throughout our lives. For example, if you've lived through family dysfunction, you may have developed the belief that you're bad, overbearing, or at fault, affecting the image you have of yourself.

A child that grew up with parents constantly down-talking at him will believe that he isn't so great after all. He will then decide to stick with the people he thinks accept him despite his unworthiness [his toxic family]. He will feel that they are doing him well by being good to him. He will likely find a partner or make friends that act like his toxic family. Children build up ideas to help them make sense of misery, even if they are untrue. Even if you weren't directly blamed for anything you were subjected to, you would internalize your family's struggle.

You may keep saying that you deserve love and respect. Still, you also subconsciously believe the contrary, which is why you may find yourself in situations where you are mistreated, thereby repeating destructive patterns.

As bad as toxic behaviors and emotionally destructive patterns are, they are very easy to get used to. After becoming accustomed to them, it takes a lot of willpower to unlearn these behaviors. It takes a lot more than just keeping away from the person or people who made you toxic to recover from toxic behavior. To properly recover, you must work on your thoughts, feelings, and behavior.

Even if you avoid some family members, you may continue to engage in toxic habits and attract toxic people. This is because the harmful effects of your toxic family haven't completely left you. You have not healed. Just walking away from them is not enough if you have unresolved feelings within your emotions. You must develop a new way of life, replacing unhealthy behaviors and mindsets with good ones. Learn new techniques for dealing with emotional outbursts while also developing important life skills.

There's a good probability they have no idea or conscience about why they do what they do. No amount of pointing out their attitudes or expressing your viewpoint, sentiments, or observations can change their minds if they refuse to listen or self-observe. As a result, while you have little control over their internal processes, you have considerable control over yourself. So why don't we make the best of what we've got and hope for brighter days ahead?

In the next chapters, you will gain strong knowledge and exercises on preventing unnecessary confrontation and avoiding making any situation worse than it already is. Understanding why your relatives behave the way they do can help you empathize and heal. Despite your bitter sentiments about what they did to you, don't be afraid to try to understand their perspective.

Chapter 3: Nobody Can Drive You Crazy If You Don't Give The Keys

66 *The more dysfunctional, the more some family members seek to control the behavior of others."*

David W. Earle

When I was younger, I used to blame all my actions and angry outbursts on the toxic behaviors of my family members. I believed that they were responsible for making me react in ridiculous ways. But as I grew older and I started discovering myself, learning, and unlearning things, I figured out that it was all me; I chose to respond how I do.

I know it's easier to seek who to blame and hold responsible for your reactions rather than be more responsible. However, you need to understand that your family members do not hold the keys to your reactions; only you do. They might choose to be toxic to you, but why do you react in toxic ways back to them? Why not react calmly? How you react is your choice. It's on you! You are solely responsible for however you decide to react. Since you are in control of your reactions, why then do you choose to hand the keys over to one who is toxic?

You can only claim to be in control of your emotions when you can control your reactions despite the toxicity around you. You need to get to a stage where you are not fazed by all the toxicity you get from your family members.

■   **How To Take Back The Keys**

Now that you know that you are the only person in charge of your emotions, how can you take back the keys and ensure you don't hand them over to your toxic family members? Follow the steps below:

Forgive Yourself

This is a very important step to gaining full control of yourself. First, you have to forgive yourself if you want to move on quickly. Forgive yourself for the times you have let others decide how you react. Forgive yourself for handing over the keys to your reactions to another person. Then you need to be at peace with yourself. Accept yourself the way you are, with all your flaws and imperfections.

I used to be angry with myself for so many reasons. Earlier in my life, I was made to believe that I was always wrong. This was because I was constantly put down for doing some things differently and did not believe in myself or my abilities.

People usually want things to go their way, and if you don't do what they believe is right, they'll make you feel like you are wrong. As a result, I used to be angry with myself for not doing things in the way my family wanted me to. However, when I set out to fully discover myself, I began to see and understand that I was doing more harm than good to myself.

Yes, it is hard to forgive yourself. But you just have to. Your healing and freedom begin when you forgive yourself.

Forgive The One Who Hurt You

Of course, they were wrong to treat you that way. You felt really bad about it. I am not disputing that the one that hurt you was wrong. I am only saying you should make an effort to forgive them. Unforgiveness is deep. It creates a deep wound in you that cannot be healed with time or medicine. The only thing that can heal this wound is consciously deciding to forgive the person who hurt you. This journey to overcoming self-blame won't happen overnight. It will go on for a long time, and the last thing you want to follow you is unnecessary baggage.

You're probably thinking about how you'd go about achieving this type of forgiveness. *"Should I apologize to them? What am I apologizing for? For being a victim of their terrible actions?"*

Calm down! Don't get yourself worked up! For the time being, you don't need to tell them anything. Your priority is to repair the wound inside of you. If you eventually achieve a higher degree of relief and feel confident enough, you can attempt the spoken apologies.

Unforgiveness will only hold you back and make your healing process slower. The one who hurt you has probably forgotten that anything of such happened. Then why do you go around with the hurt and pain? Why not let go? Why do you love unnecessary baggage?

As hard as it may seem, unforgiveness is something you need to do away with. Forgive your family for the toxicity they showed you, and forgive your friends if they were part of it. It helps you heal faster. It shows that you're becoming a better person. You drop the baggage, and you become free.

Stop Judging And Blaming Others

Do you know that it is easy to judge and blame others for making mistakes that we would have made if we were in their shoes? We need to understand that no one is perfect, not even me or you. On this journey, know that everyone you come in contact with is a work in progress, just like you. They might not have progressed as far as you have, but that doesn't mean you should judge them.

It would help if you also made an effort to refrain from criticizing and condemning people. It is not an easy task to do, but it is crucial. Everyone has flaws and fragilities, do not judge them for it. They might not even be aware that they are doing some things wrongly. Even though your parents, siblings, or other families may be deeply responsible for your vulnerability, you should try to be loving to them. Judging someone is like being the toxic person you're trying to avoid.

Do Not Be Bothered About External Opinions Or Criticism

Your new way of life may seem strange to the people around you. They would be surprised at how you react differently from what they are used to. This might make them start to criticize you or question your opinions and beliefs. Whenever I had an idea or a purpose, my brother would dissuade me somehow, attempting to ruin my opinions. His remarks weighed heavily on me as a younger brother! He always took me for granted in family gatherings or social events, taking every opportunity to denigrate my image and elevate himself among the people around us.

If you've experienced something like this, this is a time to build a wall of protection around your mind. You cannot afford to let their criticism get to you. Don't allow people's opinions to ruin your progress. You are on a journey, and you should not stop or look back until you get to where you aim to be.

It is harder to focus on being a positive person amidst toxic family members, so do not give up. If you are starting a new life, you will encounter a lot of opposition from individuals. Your loved ones and closest friends have a greater potential to hurt your feelings because they are closer to your heart. So, keep your foot on the ground.

You are not immune to criticisms; they will arise, whether within your family or from the outside. They will talk and complain but let your wall of protection be so high and strong that they can't break through it.

Never Compare Yourself

I used to feel inferior and compare my life with my brother's. He is a very intelligent individual who is very rational and analytical, yet he lacks emotional maturity and empathy. Comparison between you and your sibling or someone else can make you lose sight of your progress. You begin to only see your glass of wine as half empty instead of half full. Comparison will make you feel like you have not achieved anything. However, you forget one thing; the mere decision to avoid toxicity is already an achievement.

It might seem like the toxic people are the ones who have the best things in life, but know that you are extremely good in some areas that they are not. Each person has their own path and process to develop, and we should stick with that, using other people to observe and learn, but never to compare.

Avoid Pointless Power Struggles

Toxic people are at the center of their own universe. They often believe they are right, and they never want to admit to being wrong. They want things to go their way, and when things happen otherwise, arguments start.

It is best to avoid pointless power struggles and debates with toxic people. They are very quick to victimize themselves even when they are at fault.

Ignore what can be ignored. No matter how you want to make them understand your point of view, they will always claim to be right. So the best thing to do is avoid being in situations like these with them.

Let me share an experience with you. I left my career and studies behind and traveled to the UK with one of my brothers. Despite our arguments, my connection with my brother was always good enough for us to have fun, help, and learn from each other, but I had no idea it was toxic. So how did I find out that we shared a toxic relationship?

I found out after reading Aziz Gazipura's book "Not Nice," which walks readers through why people try to please those around them to keep them comfortable and ensure that no one dislikes them. The book made me realize that I was always trying to say and do things that pleased him. I was trying to maintain a good relationship between us because fighting wasn't an option for me.

Let me clarify this: I don't want to victimize myself with this personal story, but the things that happened my whole life are facts. I've been through a few years of reflection and therapy to understand his behavior and my reactions to him.

I was trying to figure out why I feel so horrible when I'm around him, why I feel so incompetent and inadequate when I'm around him. I had a distinct impression that his selfish remarks and haughty demeanor were suffocating me. Until it finally clicked one day, and it clicked hard!

The final drop of negativity came when we traveled to London to visit my cousin and his family, who had lived there for nearly 15 years. On the drive there, I realized that my brother was not in a good mood, so I tried to initiate talks to lighten the mood so that we could arrive relaxed and ready to enjoy the company of others. I wanted to warm up a little before being sociable and laughing naturally. I'm not sure if you can relate but think of it like warming up before a jog. This is how I make myself feel when I'm about to socialize.

At this point, I was fully aware of my brother's actions and their impact on me. He said hurtful words to me in that car, calling me dumb. He spoke with contempt and insinuated that I wasn't smart enough to understand what he was saying. This kind of insult was very unnecessary. It simply ruined my day, and I've had enough of his bad behavior. I was furious and lost all desire to see my relatives, but I had no alternative but to go.

When we got to our destination, my expression was clearly unhappy, but I didn't want to tell the entire family why. I believe you, my dear reader, are probably aware of how family members act: they can easily make quick guesses and draw hasty conclusions.

My brother laughed at me, confirmed to them that I wasn't in a great mood, and asked them to leave me alone. I may be sad about what happened between us, but I'm pleased with how I handled it over the next three days. My brother noted that I was silent and not performing normally. To him, my normal behavior was attempting to be funny, satisfying, and trying to please the people around me. So he called me, and we had a conversation.

I politely told him that I was upset about how he treats me and makes me feel worthless when I'm around him. I also suggested that he might need treatment or therapy. This triggered him. He flared up and said things about me not accepting him the way he is. Then, he quickly switched things up and made himself the victim. I suggested that he reflect on what I had said and come back to talk to me when he was ready.

Our connection steadily grew colder after that. He returned to Brazil the following year and no longer communicated with me. Of course, I miss hearing from him and having chit-chats, but in my opinion, he is using this time to assess himself and figure out why it is so difficult to communicate with him. Because, like me, other members of the family have experienced his rudeness and arrogance. What I want you to understand about my conduct is that

I'm not condemning my brother; I'm simply allowing myself to have the self-respect and time away that I need.

Come to think of it: he was the one that decided to sever ties. I only positioned myself to receive it gracefully. Once you position yourself and communicate with confidence about what you feel and what you don't want to absorb any longer, the things around you will begin to change. It might be difficult for both you and your family members to adapt to that change at first, but give yourself time. Everyone will accept the reality of things after a while. Communicate your feelings confidently and position yourself to accept the reactions and changes that will come after.

■ How To Understand Your Emotions

Understanding your emotions is a process. It is not like a switch that turns on a light bulb immediately after putting it on. The process can be likened to learning how to ride a bicycle. You will fall for the first few times, but gradually, you will gain a full hold of yourself.

I remember one time my refrigerator stopped working. I was wondering what could have gone wrong. Then I checked through the wires that connected my refrigerator to the electric socket. I noticed that the wire had cut somewhere, so it disrupted the electric flow to the refrigerator. After discovering the source of the problem, I got new wires, connected them, and my refrigerator started working well again.

I understood why the refrigerator was not working, so I was able to get a solution. This is the same way it is for your reactions. You have to understand why you react the way you do to find better ways to manage it.

Be aware of your triggers

Becoming aware of what triggers you is the first step to understanding your emotions. For example, you need to be aware of what makes you happy or sad. Have you ever had days when you were happy and content with your life, only to have your mood shift dramatically and feel like a completely different person in split seconds?

There you have it; there is something there you need to pay attention to. It might be something very simple and unnoticed that sets off your emotions. For example, someone giving you an unfriendly look, someone calling your name in a way that irritates you, or you dreamt about something that will spoil your day or possibly your week.

It also works with good things! For example, when you see an animal you love, when someone says your name in a way that makes you feel significant (yes, the same action can evoke various emotions in different people), when you hear music that brings back memories and cheers you up, or when your supervisor nods to show approval for your work, it makes you feel good about yourself, pushing you to do a better job the next day.

It's either something or someone that evokes these feelings. You can increase your self-awareness by paying close attention and reflecting on your day to discover where you are affected. Pay close attention to the triggers. You'll know how you react the next time you feel that way or find yourself in a similar situation. Then, you will be able to start playing with your emotions and driving yourself for alternative reactions and self-control. This is a process, not a remote control.

There are exercises you can engage in to help you become more aware of your triggers. Engage in the exercises daily, and they will help you strengthen your resilience and avoid instant and unwished reactions.

Exercise

Sit down at the start or end of the day and jot down some of your thoughts and emotions from the previous hours in a notebook/diary. The idea is to figure out what you're feeling and what's causing it. Then, as you reflect on the questions below, don't rush your reflection on your answers. Instead, take your time and consider it deeply. Write down your answers in the notebook/diary.

- What scenarios occurred during the day?

- How did I react in those circumstances?

- Do I feel it regularly?

- Do I react in the same way every time it happens?

- What caused me to feel that way?

- In different scenarios, how do I feel?

- Do I become enraged when I am criticized?

- Do I find it annoying when others neglect me?

- When I'm put in a situation where I have to make a quick decision, do I freeze?

Interpret Your Emotions

Now that you have a clearer understanding of how you react in different scenarios, it's time to interpret your responses to them. First, consider what to name a powerful emotion if you're having one. But don't stop there: once you've found it, attempt to think of two additional words to explain how you're feeling. You may be astonished by the range of your feelings — or by discovering a deeper emotion hidden beneath the surface.

E.g., My close friend was going through a rough patch in his marriage. He regularly referred to his wife as "angry," which made him enraged. However, as he began to look for similar terms to express his wife's emotions, he realized that she could be annoyed or impatient at times and not angry. This realization changed their relationship because he could now understand that she wasn't always angry. As a result, he was able to respond to her personal feelings and concern without becoming enraged.

This is how important interpreting your emotions can be. It can make a huge change in how you view yourself and attend to your reactions. While interpreting these emotions, ensure that you don't pass judgment on yourself for feeling the way you do.

This exercise below is solely to assist you in understanding yourself better.

Let's Dive In Deeper

Consider the following questions and write down your answers in your notebook:

- How do you behave to people when you're angry?
- How does your rage affect your attitude toward your job?
- How does it alter your perception of your own worth?
- How do you respond to others when you're overjoyed?
- How do you feel about yourself when you're happy?

Managing Your Emotions

While learning to take control of your reactions, managing your emotions is also an important step. You have to guard your emotions with all you've got. You have wide control over how you feel about your emotions, as well as how well you understand them and what you do with that knowledge. You won't have the necessary self-awareness to get the most out of life if you can't manage your emotions. Regardless, don't be too hard on yourself. We can only manage our emotions to a limited extent; we will all experience grief, anger, fear, and disappointment at some point in our lives.

Recycling

- Which of my reactions would I want to change and why?
- What can I do to control myself before taking drastic action?
- How do I feel after managing my reaction?
- Do I feel any better?

Ensure you reflect deeply on the questions in the exercises and record your progress every day for the next five weeks. This will enable you to track your thoughts, emotions, and self-awareness daily. Your notes will serve as a tool for you to learn more about yourself and have healthier strategies to deal with abusive and toxic family members. Remember to put down your views on how you will reply to your family and begin speaking with them about your boundaries whenever you have a chance.

Keep in mind that there is no one-size-fits-all approach to dealing with toxic family members; you are the expert on your personal subjects. Every day you will have an opportunity to learn about your family patterns and your emotional reactions to them. So for five weeks, repeat this previous exercise, making those questions to yourself, writing them down, and most importantly, reflecting on them.

First and second weeks, you will experience a more observative approach to the occasions around you.

Third and fourth weeks, you will have an urge to take action and start reflecting with more intensity on your emotions and reactions.

By the end of the **fifth week**, you'll have a far better understanding of what causes you irritation, anxiety, guilt, rage, sadness, or any other negative emotion that affects your health. So keep to the strategy and commit to it. Dealing with toxic relatives is never easy, but it doesn't have to be a constant in your life.

Chapter 4: Should I Stay Or Should I Go?

" *A toxic family is even worse than a toxic relationship.*"

Rohan Chouhan

If your life hasn't been how you had imagined it would be for the past few years, then it may be time for you to stop and rethink certain family relationships. Sometimes, we spend many years of our lives sacrificing our emotional and mental health in toxic relationships under the notion that we **need** to be there for certain family members, which can be draining.

I understand that cutting ties with family members can be one of the hardest things to do. For instance, who wants to be tagged as someone who doesn't speak to their family? Who wants to be the black sheep? I doubt if anyone wants to. But sometimes, drastic measures need to be taken, at least for the good of your health.

The fact remains that certain family members are toxic; if they weren't family, we wouldn't have allowed them to be part of our lives because of how they treat us. I understand that you may want to run away from such toxicity and start a new life somewhere far from negative emotions. But, sometimes, that may not be the best solution. So, if you decide to stay, how do you handle your feelings and ensure you don't get affected by their toxicity?

How Do You Handle Your Feelings?

Do you feel over-reactive? Do you feel like the current situation is stronger than you?

It can be difficult to control your emotions when dealing with toxic people; you tend to be explosive due to how they treat you. However, you need to listen and observe before acting.

If you are explosive, you will likely have the urge to vomit what rises through your stomach and come through your throat quickly – like lava in a volcano. I share your experience because I was also super over-reactive for a long time when I was younger.

I understand that holding in emotions and staying quiet to observe and think before reacting may seem impossible. Even though this can be challenging, it is possible, so don't give up easily. While pausing, it's intriguing how the awkward silence between you and the toxic person can be game-changing. When you pause to observe for just a minute, it feels like several minutes because the pause highlights their intent when they do or say something.

Your overreaction can disrupt the motive behind the message sent to you, and both of you can easily get into another round of argument. As a result, the conversation will continue with an unproductive flow of desperation to express reasons and talk without allowing a *pause* that can change many things.

I had to discuss this explosive urge because sometimes, many of us believe that the way to stop such reactions is to run away from the situation. We think running away makes dealing with toxic parents, siblings, and other relatives easier. So we choose to run away and live without the negative impact such people have on us.

Now, the question is, what is the best decision to make? To stay and deal with their toxicity that involves everyday challenges, or to run away someplace where you can have more peace of mind?

It's important to note that not everyone has the opportunity to leave, and sometimes, running away may not always be the solution. Therefore, if you are among those that decided to stay, what can you do to cope with the situation?

■ To Stay or Leave: If I Stay, What Should I Do?

Even though you choose to stay with your toxic relatives, it's very important that you get emotionally detached for your own sanity. Toxic relationships can be emotionally draining and can affect your physical and emotional health.

Of course, it's difficult to emotionally detach yourself from someone or people you have a strong bond with. However, emotional detachment seems to be the only way to protect your emotional and mental health from toxic relatives. But before I delve into how you can achieve this, it is important to know what emotional detachment is.

Emotional detachment is when you disconnect from someone emotionally. It simply means you want to end all emotional ties with someone.

Now, how do you stay emotionally detached from someone you care about? Below are ways to detach yourself emotionally from a toxic family member. Ensure you practice them, and you'll start seeing changes gradually.

Find A Reason Why You Want The Emotionally Detachment

Avoiding a toxic relative doesn't mean you have to stop all communications with the person or start behaving badly to the person. However, you need to have a point that takes out all emotions from you toward this person. Think of it as your reason for the detachment and continue reminding yourself every day that it's because of that reason you want to detach yourself (emotionally) from the person completely.

Let's assume that you are currently seeking a reason for why you want to detach yourself from a relative. Maybe this person has become very toxic to you, they have become a different person, and they constantly belittle you whenever you are around them. These are already good enough reasons for you to consider detaching yourself from them emotionally. However, ensure you don't disrespect them while finding your reasons; don't stoop to their level.

Don't Allow Them To Come Too Close To You

Taking a step back and analyzing how close a person is to you can help you detach yourself from them emotionally. If you get too close to a toxic relative and make them your confidant, they will use what they know against you. Instead, don't disclose all aspects of your life, don't tell them your plans, and avoid hanging out with them frequently.

It's good to have people around you whom you can share secrets with. However, it's better to do this with someone you trust and who makes you feel good, not the other way around.

Courteous Disagreements

You might feel tempted to nod and grin to avoid an angry reaction. This may appear as the safest option, but it encourages the toxic relative to regard you as a dumb fellow and exploit you. Instead, you can try courteous disagreements by saying, "I have a different take on the scenario." Then recount what transpired. Don't make any accusations; stick to the facts. If the dispute becomes too heated, you can choose to remain silent after you've spoken your truth.

Invest In Self-Development

You may be wondering what self-development has got to do with emotional detachment. Building yourself can help shift your focus to better things instead of giving them your attention.

Use your spare time to learn how to cook, buy a pet, go for a vacation, and do anything fun! This allows you to become better at something, and you won't have to depend on people to achieve this.

Have you been thinking of getting into a university? Do you have a dream job you are aiming for? Or do you have a particular skill you want to learn? Use this opportunity and put your heart and mind into what you want to achieve, and you will notice that you've gradually moved your focus from the toxic relative to things that improve your growth.

Start Taking Small Steps

You can't emotionally detach yourself from someone overnight; it will take some time and effort from you. However, this shouldn't discourage you. You just need to start with a step to see results, regardless of how small it is. Start by getting rid of the things that always remind you of them. For example, you can delete their messages or mute their social media notifications so you wouldn't have to often see things about them.

Forgive And Move On

To detach yourself from a toxic relative, you may need to forgive them for their actions. By forgiving them, you are letting go of the reason making you feel stuck and unable to move on. With forgiveness, over time, you will find yourself forgetting them.

Think about the future; you might not see this person in your future. So, forgive them now and find a way to deal with tasks without involving them. This way, you can learn to be independent. Regardless of your past with the person, let go and think about how beautiful the future will be.

Seek Help From Therapists

I understand that emotional detachment can be difficult and overwhelming. Also, certain circumstances will take a toll on your emotions. For example, emotionally detaching yourself from a toxic family you've lived with all your life can make you feel miserable, alone, and confused because you've known them for so long. This can be a complicated situation. Therefore, you need to seek help from a professional if it affects your feelings and productivity. A therapist will give you unbiased help. But hold it shallow for now because we will get into what therapy can make in the next chapters.

And that's it! These are ways you can emotionally detach yourself from toxic relatives. Know that emotional detachment may seem bad to people who aren't in your shoes. However, remember that your emotions are what make you human. Sometimes you need to use those emotions intelligently because if you don't, toxic people will use them against you and misuse the power you've given them. If you can intelligently use your emotions, you can make better decisions and maintain a healthy distance from them.

As I've mentioned earlier, emotional detachment is something you need to practice, and gradually, you will master it and become stronger and capable of being in control. This can be your way out of worry, chaos, and the increased emotional pain you've been experiencing. Start where you are now, and you'll see that detachment is like liberation.

Despite being effective, emotional detachment may not be enough to free yourself from the shackles of emotional abuse from your relatives. So if you notice that you can't cope, cutting ties may be the next action.

Cutting Ties With A Toxic Person

Cutting ties with a toxic relative can be an awkward situation. The idea of choosing between yourself and family members sucks! However, this is reality, and choosing to remain in a relationship with them may harm your physical and emotional health.

Ultimately, the only way you can truly heal is to remove yourself from a family that abuses you and is toxic to your health.

Toxic family members can disrupt your life and affect your relationships with others. They exhibit behaviors towards you such as:

- Blaming
- Lying
- Overreacting
- Creating chaos and drama
- Criticizing
- Manipulating
- Belittling
- Gaslighting
- Ignoring
- Refusing compromise
- Cursing, yelling, and name-calling
- Gossiping and speaking ill behind your back
- Making crazy requests
- Playing victim
- Ruining special occasions
- Avoid owning up to their behaviors
- Never apologizes, and if they do, it's always fake
- Always seeking help but never available to help you

- ○ Always claiming that their right
- ○ Have no interest in your growth
- ○ Creating only stress, pain, and anxiety

Of course, people can change their ways, but toxic relatives hardly do that. They are not self-aware and hardly take responsibility for their actions. Instead of focusing on changing them, rather focus on yourself.

So, how can you cut ties with toxic relatives?

The following are ways you can cut ties with your toxic relatives and protect your mental state.

Know That It Won't Be An Easy Task

Cutting ties is a grieving process; ensure you take the time to grieve and heal for what you're about to do. For example, you may feel bad when the holidays roll in or during your birthday, and they aren't around you. Plan ahead by practicing self-care routines such as meditation, journaling, and self-affirmations. These should encourage you whenever you feel overwhelmed and lonely. Open yourself up and release those harmful feelings you have in you. Releasing them leads to your healing.

Avoid Contact

Avoid contacting them via emails, calls, or visits. You may be worried that regardless of their actions, they are still family, and you shouldn't be mean to them. However, it would help if you avoided contact, for now, at least to heal. You need the time for yourself to gain a better perspective. And if you must contact them if there is a significant event that took place and they need to know, you can send an email to let the family member know that you're moving to another place, you're getting married, you have a baby, or you lost someone. Regardless of their response, focus on keeping your messages positive.

Focus On Who You Are And Who You Have

By maintaining your values, you're focusing on yourself while having a good support system of friends, colleagues, and even other family members who aren't toxic can make cutting ties easier. So, define your values, what you stand for, and the people who support you.

Don't Pretend

At this point, you don't need to minimize your feelings and thoughts by pretending everything is okay when it's not. So instead of keeping quiet and avoiding some uncomfortable conversations, speak up! Don't cower in fear when their behavior hurts you badly. It will only get worse if you don't speak up.

Ways To Protect Yourself From Toxic Family Members

By avoiding confrontations with toxic people, you are doing yourself good. Unfortunately, certain conflicts in life are simply too big to overlook. No matter how hard you attempt to make them go away or appear smaller than they are, the agony and suffering continue to grow until there is an enormous eruption.

Certain situations will not benefit from the instability that confrontation may bring. This is especially true when it comes to close family and to set the limits, you need to feel safe and happy. If you have many toxic family relations, a big sign of maturity is learning how to cut them off and deal with the inevitable tension that comes with it.

Set Boundaries

Setting boundaries is an easy way to cut ties with your toxic relations. However, it may be difficult to set boundaries for people whose household doesn't respect or value boundaries. I recommend that you express your demands and feelings openly and firmly. You could also learn to keep a safe distance from toxic relatives. While some people choose to cut ties completely, others try to improve the situation by limiting their interaction with toxic family members and taking measures to safeguard their mental well-being.

Know what you want out of the relationship. This should help you determine the boundaries you wish to establish. For example, you can avoid letting them into your personal space. In addition, you need to refrain from inquiring about their personal lives; only share information regarding the family's most important business.

Avoid Arguments

Try to avoid arguments at all costs. Toxic people like engaging their victims in arguments to divert their attention away from true concerns. It's easy for them to turn the tables on you, blame you for their destructive behaviors, and never accept responsibility for their actions.

Toxic people tend to see themselves as victims in every circumstance. If they make a mistake, they blame someone else or tell a story that portrays them more favorably. Your best reaction should be to avoid getting into heated arguments with them.

Don't Give Your All

In a toxic family setting, the victim will always give while the abuser is on the receiving end. It might even seem like their mental well-being is dependent on you. You may appreciate your relationship with this individual, but don't put your health at risk by offering too much support. Giving and taking are both necessary components of a healthy partnership – you assist and receive too. Ensure you have the mental energy to address your own needs. This may not be the case if you give everything to someone who doesn't reciprocate.

Stand Your Ground

It might be difficult to stick to a decision or cut ties completely. However, don't back down if you decide to say "No." This could be difficult, especially if they use a dramatic reaction to gain their way. Know that the more you learn to say "no" to them, the easier it will become. If you can't detach yourself from them emotionally, then it's time to cut ties with them physically. Make it plain that you are no longer interested in being with them.

Don't Feel Guilty

Even if you know you didn't do anything wrong, toxic people might make you feel like you've done something wrong. They may attempt to twist your comments and turn others against you. You might even start second-guessing yourself and ruminating about what you might have done wrong. Keep in mind that their actions have nothing to do with you. Reiterate your boundaries and make an effort not to take their hostility personally.

To relax, take a few deep breaths. Toxic people are concerned with themselves and what they desire. They may blame you or others for their difficulties and show little concern for your feelings or needs.

■ Steps Towards Forgiveness: How Will This Work In My Case?

As you move on, you need to learn how to forgive your toxic relative that has caused you great pain. Forgiveness is an important step so you are able to move forward. Even though it's hard, it is achievable. But how can you achieve this?

The following are steps you can utilize to forgive a toxic family member that has wronged you.

Forgiving Isn't Forgetting

When you forgive your relative, it doesn't mean that you forget what they've done to you. It's very easy for toxic family members to pretend that nothing happened after they've hurt you. This can brew resentment in you, which has a negative impact. When you forgive them, you aren't saying, "It's okay for you to hurt me. I'll choose to pretend it didn't happen." Instead, what you are saying is, "You've hurt me, and it's so wrong that I've been affected by your actions. However, I choose not to take revenge."

Write A Letter

I find this particular step very interesting because writing is one activity I enjoy. I've come to realize the healing powers of written words. You can try it too by writing your toxic relative a letter and expressing how you feel. No matter how bad they've made you feel, you don't need to trade blames or make accusations.

Do you want to know the trick to this activity? After writing the letter, you aren't sending it to the person. Instead, it's meant to be a way of releasing old and stuck emotions that aren't serving you. This will help you forgive them.

Know That Their Behavior is a Reflection of Their Issues

It's almost impossible to please a relative who treats you and other people around badly. How they treat you is usually due to their insecurities. For example, if a family member always belittles you and makes bad comments about your appearance, there is a possibility that they are unhappy about their appearance and are picking on you to help them validate their negative assumptions about life. If you understand that how they treat people reflects their emotional state, you can forgive them for their actions.

Be Empathic

Now that you understand that your relative is treating you badly due to their emotional state, you might need to consider having genuine empathy for them. For example, when you start empathizing with someone who constantly talks down on you, you may rationalize why they treat you badly.

Their actions may be traced to their childhood when their parents constantly talked down on them or belittled them. So, it is the result of their upbringing. Also, their actions may result from an underlying mental illness, which makes it not their fault. Regardless, ensure you are empathic towards them – don't overdo it.

Seek Therapy And Direction

I know I've mentioned this earlier, but we shouldn't underrate the potential benefits of therapy. Therapy is for everyone, especially those dealing with complex family dynamics. A professional can give you insight and advice on how to forgive those who have hurt you and show you ways to manage difficult relationships.

Finally, if you struggle with certain people in your life, you need to brace up and know that not all relationships (family or not) will work. Even though people around you seem to have the perfect family, many people out there deal with wounds that aren't on the surface. I've come to learn that a shared family tree doesn't suggest that parents and siblings will act lovingly. However, by forgiving the people that caused you pain, you'll gain the freedom to let go and find healing for yourself.

Chapter 5: How to Help Stop the Vicious Cycle of Self-Sabotage and Self-Destruction

 *Love them from a distance. Pray for them, wish them well, but don't allow them to abuse you."*

Kimber Waul

While it may seem shocking, it is common to see people undermine their own plans and abandon their goals. As a result, they hinder their success and sabotage themselves. You may find it surprising that anyone would want to sabotage themselves, but let me ask. What is your New Year's resolution? Months after making resolutions, plans, and setting beautiful goals, have you been able to achieve anything? Are you still working on it, or have you abandoned the resolutions while making promises and taking a mental note to complete them next year?

So many people embark on New Year's goals and resolutions with great determination and the hope of completing them to improve their lives and the things around them for the coming year. However, it is common for about 80% of the people who had made plans which they promised not to fail would have abandoned everything by the beginning of February, hoping to try again next year and do better.

Funny to find yourself as a firsthand culprit? You're not alone; we've all been guilty of trailing off and abandoning our intentions and goals. Our resolutions and plans are disrupted in many ways, and one of the main reasons is self-sabotage.

Failing to accomplish goals, abandoning plans, and procrastinating may not seem harmful. However, consistent self-sabotaging can build up into destructive, harmful behaviors, negatively impacting almost every aspect of our lives, such as our personal or professional lives.

This chapter addresses the prevalent reasons people tend to self-sabotage and who is responsible for the action. Is it you or someone else?

But first, let's discuss self-sabotage.

■ What is Self-Sabotage?

Self-sabotage refers to people ruining or harming themselves physically, emotionally, or mentally by deliberately impeding their own success. They undermine their personal goals, intentions, and values.

A psychological definition will attribute self-sabotage as a behavioral dysregulation, which could either be a conscious or an unconscious action depending on the awareness level of the individual. A good example of a conscious act of self-sabotage is when a patient treating lung disease decides to keep smoking harmful tobacco. On the other hand, an unconscious act of self-sabotage could happen when an individual is undermining a personal goal without knowing it.

Self-sabotage can also be defined as cognitive dissonance. Cognitive dissonance is when we experience internal imbalance because our thoughts, attitudes, values, and beliefs are inconsistent and do not align. This internal imbalance can cause discomfort leading us to keep changing our behaviors, words, or beliefs or procrastinating on our goals and reframing our values.

Knowing the harm self-sabotage can cause in our lives, it would seem unlikely that anyone would attempt to sabotage themselves consciously, yet we do, even when the consequences are damaging. When we experience protracted self-sabotage, it depletes our motivation and drive to accomplish anything leaving us sad, nervous, and with low or damaged self-esteem.

■ Possible Causes Why People Self-Sabotage?

Self-Sabotage: Conscious vs. Unconscious

Some people consciously sabotage their actions even when they know the consequences, yet they don't care about the outcome. On the other hand, some unconscious acts can lead to self-sabotage. For example, a person who misses the deadline for a job. From the outside, it would seem like they ran out of time while doing their best. However, the truth is that they missed the deadline due to the fear of failure. The act of self-sabotage occurs when they miss the deadline. Hence, they impede their growth, thwart their effort, and fail to move the company forward.

Either consciously or unconsciously, there are myriad reasons why people adopt destructive behavior that impede their own development. For example, it could be due to childhood experiences, issues from a past relationship, or presently coping with cognitive dissonance problems, which we will be discussing below.

Trauma

Trauma is one of the main causes of self-sabotage, especially a childhood traumatic experience where a child is violated or abused by someone they trust. Such a child would grow up seeing the world as an unsafe place where people cannot be trusted and see themselves as undeserving of love or anything good, leading them to self-sabotage.

Relationships Difficulties

If you've experienced a relationship where you get put down a lot, and your opinions and feelings don't count, you might still feel oppressed and vulnerable. Your partner (probably now an ex) could have exposed you to different forms of abuse and left you devastated with words like, *"I'm way better off moving forward without someone like you in my life."*

Now you're in a different relationship with someone great and adorable. Still, you can't help but feel insecure, and you want to keep another relationship as a backup and even cheat on them for no reason. Your last relationship(s) could have imprinted fear in your mind. Therefore, the fear of getting hurt could make you feel you're not good enough and drive you to sabotage the good thing you have going.

Self-sabotage in a family setting is mostly caused when you've experienced things that will make you have a sense of low self-esteem, insecurity, fear of trusting and opening up to another person, and unhealthy beliefs.

Low Self-Esteem

People with low self-esteem have a negative self-image and risk self-sabotaging their goals. Their actions make them vulnerable to accepting and affirming negative beliefs about themselves. Hence, they are likely to self-sabotage whenever they're close to success; they become uncomfortable because they don't believe they are worth it.

They've become used to the idea of failing since they've been made to believe they're failures all their lives. In some cases, they develop a low self-image and tell themselves they'll fail at everything they do and believe it.

Cognitive Dissonance

People with self-sabotaging behavior usually struggle with cognitive dissonance. This means they struggle with internal imbalance due to holding too many conflicting beliefs, ideas, and values. As humans, we need balance and consistency between our actions and beliefs to maintain self-confidence.

For example, you fell in love with someone exceptional, but since you're from a dysfunctional family, you've witnessed your parents abuse themselves during their numerous fights. Growing up with such a background, you no longer believe in a harmonious, stable, and loving relationship. So, if your intention is to get married to this great person, while you don't believe in such a relationship, there's a high probability that you'll pull a self-sabotaging stunt.

It could also happen in a work-related environment where someone will sabotage their progress because they don't feel they are worthy of success. They could miss the meeting by getting too drunk the night before and impede their own success.

Self-sabotage is a destructive behavior that can lead to liquor or drug abuse, gambling, and self-inflicted injury.

Toxic Shame

Toxic shame is a depressing belief of worthlessness. When people treat you poorly without respect, you may begin to have a low opinion of yourself with this treatment and accept them as a belief about yourself. This is especially so if you were exposed to poor treatment as a child or in your teenage years. You develop this belief when people close to you embarrass you at every opportunity making you feel worthless.

This entrenched emotion will influence your self-confidence and affect how you see yourself – as worthless.

People feel shame at some point in their lives, but how does this shame become toxic?

Like everyone, you probably have felt shame at different times. You can feel shame that lasts for hours, days, or weeks. However, shame becomes toxic when you're constantly being told you're not adequate or like your peers. The result of these emotions is negative self-talk you begin to see as the truth about yourself.

For most people that suffer from toxic shame, it starts from the type of feedback they received when they were younger, usually from a parent or people close to them.

Hannah was a friend I met a few years ago who was deep into toxic self-shame and always wore a sad frown. We met in a group where people with a tendency to self-sabotage gather and discuss their experiences and challenges. I remember the first time Hannah spoke during one of our sessions; I could feel how sad and drained she sounded.

After some time, we talked, and I understood that she was also a victim of a toxic family. As an orphan, she bounced from one relative to another before she was 13 years old, and after that, she settled with an uncle, where the family treated her as their maid. She was always talked down on and never had the voice to say anything or express her pain.

Several years of being constantly told she wouldn't amount to anything affected Hannah's personality and her perspective about life in general. She no longer had the drive to do anything for herself. As a result, she lost the ability to take the initiative and was constantly second-guessing all her actions and even her thoughts until she got help.

If you've been in a similar situation and you were constantly told or rebuked in certain ways, such as:

- "You always get things wrong; why are you acting dumb?"
- "You're not and will never be as good as others."
- "What kept you? You are so lazy."

You might start believing these words when told often, and you'll start shaming yourself because you already accepted it. Holding such beliefs of shamefulness and worthlessness can harm your physical and mental health.

Rejection or neglect

Nobody wants to be left neglected or rejected by a parent or loved one. However, feeling rejected or neglected can make you struggle with negative self-image and low self-esteem. Constantly experiencing such negative emotions can cause people to self-sabotage their relationships in an effort to be invulnerable to neglect and rejection.

Common Ways People Self-Sabotage

Although I have given some examples of how people self-sabotage, mental health experts believe there are three common ways people self-sabotage. By identifying them, changes and lifestyle adjustments can begin to take effect.

■ Procrastination

One common trait among people who self-sabotage is procrastination. You procrastinate as a way of telling others that you're not ready or perhaps never ready to deliver a favorable outcome. The underlying problem here could be fear of failing, disappointing others, or the fear of succeeding because you don't know how to handle success.

■ Perfectionism

Setting your bar too high, with many expectations, and imposing impossible standards for yourself could lead to setbacks and delays, causing more harm than good. Though it may seem like a good strategy to aim very high, it could impede success when it becomes perfectionism(wanting to achieve your goals without any hitch).

There are too many uncertainties in the world, and things usually don't go as we plan. For a perfectionist, this will be their undoing. They end up with complicated feelings and emotions such as shame and a sense of defeat and could even get depressed. They'll feel like their public image has been ruined by letting the people around them down.

■ Self-Medication

As I've mentioned before, people who self-sabotage could be struggling with a conflict between their beliefs and actions. So, to win their inner battle of wanting to become successful vs. the voice in their head telling them they can't make it, they result in the use of drugs, self-injury, or alcohol to soothe themselves.

■ Self-sabotage and Self-destruction in Relationships

There are several reasons why people sabotage relationships, so before we can make any changes in our lives, we need to first understand the complex origins of sabotage. For example, sabotage in a relationship could be picking fights when there's nothing to fight about, settling with someone you know you're not compatible with, or not opening up and fully committing to relationships.

Other examples of relationship sabotage are:

- ○ Chronic mistrust

- Losing yourself and your personality in a relationship
- Constantly criticizing your partner
- Silencing 'the self'
- Holding grudges
- Focusing on other people's flaws instead of the relationship
- Channeling your energy on less important things and letting your relationship suffer

Besides these intentional or conscious examples of self-sabotage in relationships, there are other subtle forms of relationship sabotage. These forms of self-sabotage are mostly done without realization, **at least not on a conscious level**, and some examples are:

- Chasing someone who is not interested in you
- Belittling yourself, insisting you're not good, attractive, or worthy enough
- Trying to please others by changing yourself even if it hurts

- Being aggressive or displaying hostile behavior that repels people
- Wallowing in self-deprecating pity

The severity of these maladaptive behaviors varies from one individual to another. For some people, it might be mild without being an immediate threat, but for others, these behaviors are dangerous and can cause severe harm.

Self-destructive behaviors

People with self-sabotaging behaviors are prone to behave or engage in self-destructive acts, such as:

- Drug abuse
- Alcohol abuse
- Physical or emotional abuse
- Self-harm and injury
- Inflicting childhood traumatic experiences on others
- Friends who self-injure
- Self-isolation and low self-esteem

The first step to dealing with these behaviors is understanding them and the ones you experience.

Then you can work on healing from your past and work on your sense of "SELF," including having open communication with people around you.

How to Stop and Avoid Self-Sabotage

Why do people repeat the damaging act of self-sabotage when they know it is detrimental? Because people tend to repeat what gets rewarded. People who self-sabotage indulge in this behavior because they need to fill a void in their lives.

To stop the chain of self-destructive behaviors, we need to learn about these voids and consciously train ourselves to adapt to new behaviors.

It is one thing to engage in self-sabotage, but it's a totally different affair to admit it and accept help. However, if you're already working with a therapist, I will boldly tell you to heed their advice and guidance as someone who has passed through similar situations.

Meanwhile, here are some other pointers to help you avoid these negative behaviors and stop you from causing more harm to yourself or the people around you.

It requires effort to self-sabotage

Self-sabotaging acts take a lot of work, which is time-consuming and resource-demanding. According to a study by researchers at Indiana University, people who are more productive in the morning (early birds) self-sabotage in the morning, while those who are more productive at night (night owls) self-sabotage in the night.

This means they sabotage their goals or performances not because they are tired but when they are at their performance peak. Hence, self-sabotage demands work and effort to carry out. It requires a lot of energy to keep up this behavior with the damaging outcome. Channel your energy into completing your goals instead of taking the pain of self-sabotage.

Find the root causes

Do specific patterns in your life make you behave a certain way? Do you feel susceptible to sabotaging your good efforts? When did you notice this behavior? Do you act to sabotage your good efforts when you're close to success (work) or when you find yourself in a good place (relationship)?

Self-sabotage could stem from anywhere and at any point in our lives. Some parents, ignorant of their actions and thinking they're helping their child, would repeatedly tell their kids not to dream or think big. For example, they could tell a kid, *"You need to work like every member of the family, so don't even think you'll be attending college."*

Finding what your root cause is will point you towards a lasting solution.

Stop procrastinating

Procrastination is one trait that most people who self-sabotage share. It is easier to put off things that are important to you. That way, you won't have to endure the battle between your beliefs and actions. For example, you might find it easier on your emotions to put off something important to you than achieving it since you were told as a kid you'd never reach it.

The imbalance between what you've learned for years and the place you are now could cause severe discomfort. So, consciously or not, you self-sabotage.

Although you could procrastinate for several reasons, you still need to take charge of your life and fix your habits. To do that, you need to rephrase your internal dialogue, learn to forgive yourself, and accept yourself.

Learn self-compassion

No one is perfect, and everyone makes mistakes. But, even if it seems you've made the worst mistakes in the world, there's always room for redemption. Therefore, accept that you're human and learn from your mistake – but don't get caught up or stuck in it. Continuing your journey with self-compassion will open up a new perspective on life, providing you with insights to accept and love yourself.

Practice mindfulness

Learning how to observe your thoughts will keep you from straying off into self-sabotage. Practicing mindfulness and meditation can help you stay in the moment and be tethered to reality with your thoughts fully under control. You'll get rational answers when you notice your thoughts and question them. This powerful method can keep you from reacting to negative emotions like shame or self-doubt.

Talk to someone close to you when you're feeling shame and your internal dialogue is not enough to pull you out. Shame thrives in dark secretive places where no one has access. By talking to someone, you're shining a light on the emotions growing in the dark, and they'll start fading away. Mindfulness keeps you alert and aware of your emotions.

Seek support

Like the popular saying, *"no one is an island,"* don't isolate yourself and repel everyone from you. Seeking a support network can boost your sense of belonging and give you a channel to talk things out and share.

Stop being a perfectionist

Sometimes the simple things are the things we lack the most. Stop overthinking things, wanting every detail and everything to be perfect, just how you have envisioned it in your head. Self-sabotaging people are sometimes perfectionists. They begin to crumble when things go wrong, thinking they're the worst people since they've disappointed the people around them.

You don't have to aim for things to be perfect. Instead, aim for excellence. Implement small improvements, make progress even if it's small, and you'll accomplish your desired goals.

■ Treatment: Therapeutically Strategies To Stop Self-Sabotage And Self-Destruction

People who self-sabotage or self-destruct can get help for the various problems they face, including drug and alcohol abuse, self-isolation, aggressive outbursts, anger episodes, binge eating, and self-harm.

Below are therapies that can help those with self-destructive behavior:

- **Cognitive-behavioral therapy (CBT)**
  This involves therapeutic techniques effective in alleviating cognitive dissonance. CBT techniques help you change your negative internal monologues and thought patterns and improve general well-being.

- **Dialectical behavior therapy (DBT)**
  This therapy is effective when dealing with problems related to intense emotions, such as impulse control issues, chronic self-isolation

issues, impulsive behaviors, and difficulty associating or getting along with other people. This therapy will teach you how to control your emotions and properly handle situations better.

Although there is no defined method of addressing self-sabotage issues during therapy sessions, every individual is plagued with unique underlying reasons for self-sabotage. However, these treatments are effective in helping people deal with issues related to success and growth, especially pointing to their underlying core beliefs and ambivalence.

Several therapeutic interventions are effective for acceptance, commitment, and working through inconsistency and damaging mindsets. In addition, some approaches help alter and balance the relationship between your thoughts and core beliefs and eventually let go and open up.

Self-sabotage can negatively affect your daily life and can have crippling effects, consider seeing a professional if you notice that you're self-sabotaging yourself.

Chapter 6: Secret Tips To Cope With Family Gatherings: Events, Celebrations, and Funerals

> 66 *Family is supposed to be our safe haven. Very often, it's the place where we find the deepest heartache."*

Iyanla Vanzant

I was very excited when my mum told me my cousin would be getting married soon. I was so happy because she has been through a lot and deserves to be happy. She was recovering from a messy divorce, and we all knew she deserved a good man. So we were happy that she was finally getting what she needed.

As her wedding date drew closer, I began to lose interest in attending the wedding ceremony; the excitement was no longer there. This was surprising because I was truly happy for my cousin and wished her well. I really wanted to be there for her. However, I didn't understand why I felt this way until the wedding day.

I was driving to the venue, and my heart started beating fast. I developed a headache and began to sweat. I became mentally unsettled. Then it dawned on me that I loved my cousin, but I dreaded the company of the rest of the family that was going to be present at the wedding. I was going to meet uncles, aunts, grandparents, and other family members who never mind their business.

Toxic family members can drain your energy, this is real!

Have you ever been so bubbly and happy, but once you get to a family gathering, your happiness seems to diminish gradually? Do you feel your heart beating fast when you know you are going to a family gathering? Have you ever felt anxious and wondered how it would feel when you stay in the same place with family members? Are you already overwhelmed by just imagining how frustrating it would be?

Well, I understand how you may feel because I've had the same experience.

I am not a very social person. Going out to parties and meeting people is not something I love to do. I would rather stay in bed watching a movie or reading a good book than hanging out with people who will only make me feel bad. It is hard! Having to deal with all these people, their different thoughts, all their opinions, and answering annoying questions.

Like I said earlier, I have to do a warm-up to emotionally prepare myself when meeting and interacting with certain family members. As much as I can, I avoid occasions where I have to sit and talk for long periods. However, when it comes to important family gatherings like a cousin's birthday or a sibling's wedding, I can't escape it. Most of the time, I needed to be present.

I love my family, and I want to be there to celebrate with them. But, at the same time, I have to put my mental health into good consideration. That is why I had to develop some coping strategies to help me and ensure my mental health wasn't affected by their presence. These strategies help me have fun with my family while keeping my inner peace in check.

■ 8 Tips For Coping With Family Gathering

The tips below will greatly help you if you have to be at a family gathering and don't want to return home looking gloomy and sad.

1. Look At The Bright Side

Your experience with your family members would naturally put your guards up against them. This is why before meeting them, you already feel overwhelmed by the thought of having to see them. No one is completely bad. There is still some form of goodness in your toxic family members.

Focusing on the positive side of your family members will help you relate with them freely.

Think of all the characteristics you admire about your family members before meeting with them, and mentally separate who they are as a person from their toxic conduct—focusing on the positive rather than the negative will help you deal with the activities that annoy you. This is because your stress level will not increase before you see them, making it easier for you to engage happily with them.

2. Determine The Duration Of Your Visit

Before going to any celebration, event, or gathering with your relatives, decide how long you will be there. How much time can you spend with your family members that will be healthy for your mind? Just an hour or two isn't such a bad idea for me. However, it might be much or less for you, so decide what's appropriate.

From my research and experience, spending a shorter time with family members is more manageable than spending a long time with them.

Removing toxic family members from your life is almost impossible. Instead of missing out on important family events, keep your visit brief. You are not mandated to stay for the entire event.

Notice how you're feeling. Remember to check in with yourself if you're spending a lot of time with a toxic family member. Take note of any tension in your body and use some soothing practices to help you get through difficult times. For example, you can take breaks by going to the restroom to spend some time alone or drinking a glass of water. You have the right to excuse yourself from the event if you've reached your emotional breaking point.

3. Reassess Your Boundaries

Reassessing your boundaries before you go to any family gathering is very important. This will help you decide which toxic behaviors you will address and which ones you will ignore. As much as it might hurt, not every toxic behavior requires a reaction from you.

Some behaviors are better left unaddressed. This does not mean that you condone their actions. It just implies that attending family gatherings will be a lot easier for you if you ignore some petty behaviors and don't engage them.

4. Create Internal Boundaries

Do you remember what I said about building a mental wall of protection so high that no one can pass through it? This is where it comes in handy. Creating internal boundaries involves devising strategies for letting go of the hurt so that the toxicity does not penetrate your mind. The toxicity hits the wall of protection and bounces away, out of your mind.

Internal boundaries can be developed by thinking of some positive affirmations. Words like, *"I am good enough; I am smart."* These are words that you can use when interacting with a toxic person. Say it repeatedly till it sticks to your subconscious.

5. Establish Ground Rules

I noticed that I could not have conversations about sports cars without it becoming a heated argument between my brother and me. I didn't particularly appreciate how my brother always made a fuss, so I thought of a way to avoid the conversation. Whenever I met him at a family gathering, I sent a text saying, *"I really appreciate having conversations with you, but whenever we get together, we tend to argue about sports cars a lot. Because of this, I think this topic should be avoided"*. This gave him an idea of what wasn't to be spoken about to ensure that the occasion went smoothly without anyone getting emotional.

Your family members may be unaware that their actions are bothering you, especially if no one has told them. Telling them which of their actions bother you might backfire, and they will most likely flare up, but it's still worth a go. There's no need to keep repeating oneself if it doesn't work the first time.

If you are aware of any topic or action that might trigger you or your family member, do well to inform them ahead of time to stay off the topic. For example, if you do not like people touching your belongings, tell them to stay off your stuff politely. Good communication can help you have a relaxing and enjoyable time with your family.

6. Avoid Personal Questions

Toxic family members have a way of using your personal information to hurt you emotionally. This is one reason why you should avoid personal questions. They might feel like they are family and need to know everything about you but be wary. Filter the information you give to them. If they do not have your information, they can't use it against you.

At a point in my life, I had to stop attending family functions to discover myself and keep my mental health in check fully. I wasn't married, but I had plans to. My aunt asked whether I was in a relationship, and I innocently told her I wasn't. It wasn't until later, when I argued with an uncle, that I heard she had gone around telling people that I've never had a girlfriend and saying I was confused about my gender.

It's just funny how family members make a lot of crazy speculations about you and expect you to be okay with it. If someone is overly curious orFor example, suppose someone inquires about your financial situation. In that case, you can deflect the question by saying, "That is a very personal question. I'm trying to add more positivity to my life, so why don't we talk about something more fun?". This way, you're politely avoiding the topic. You could also say, *I appreciate your concern, but this topic is off-limits."*

Don't be surprised that they might try to press on and insist that you answer the question. Simply emphasize your point and let them know you will not discuss your private life. If they persist, leave the environment, and let them know you don't want to discuss the subject.

7. Don't Snap

The worst mistake you can make around toxic family members at an event or gathering is snap at them. It would escalate so quickly that you might be unable to handle it. They would come at you so bad that you would be at the losing end. It is even worse when the person you snapped at is older.

If you sense that the conversation is heading in an awful direction, take a brief pause and say, *"This discussion is getting heated. I'd like to have some time to myself."* If the conversation has been too overwhelming for you and you'd prefer to end it, say, *"It's been a pleasure talking with you. For the time being, let's end it here."* You can also say, *"I'm feeling a little drained. Let's talk about this at a later time."*

It's preferable to end a terrible conversation with a tough family member since the more you chat, the less productive the dialogue becomes, and the dispute escalates. Explain to the person that you will not engage in a scathing conversation, and stick to your word.

Engaging yourself in heated arguments and fights is just you telling them that they still have access to your reactions. You should air your opinions respectfully, whether they are being disrespectful or not. You are not like them, so be respectful and don't snap.

8. Call A Friend

Having a trusted friend come with you to a family gathering might help you get along well. Family members try to put on their best act when there are strangers around, so this might help calm the air a little bit. Apart from that, you can call your friend aside and vent whenever you start to feel overwhelmed. This prevents you from snapping at your family.

Just in case it is a private family gathering and you are not allowed to bring friends, have a friend you can call to talk to. Let your friend know beforehand that they should expect a call from you. Also, do not forget to prepare your friend for the nature of the call. This way, your friend would not be caught off guard.

▪ 3 Tips To Note When Attending Funerals Or Memorial Service

Knowing whether or not to attend the funeral or memorial ceremony and how to act can be tough, especially if you have a complicated relationship with the person who died or with the surviving family.

Though there are no hard and fast rules for handling complicated relationships at a funeral or memorial ceremony, it's usually best to trust your instincts. It's also vital to consider other people's feelings and remember that having other people's support at a funeral may make a mourning family feel loved and cared for.

The following are tips to note when deciding whether to attend a family member's funeral.

1. Reach Out For Clarification

Ask! Many emotions might occur when a family member you weren't on good terms with passes away. You may want to attend the funeral or memorial ceremony but are conflicted. You may be unsure how others will react to your presence.

If you're worried that your decision whether to attend or not or bring children or not would upset particular family members, reach out to them before the service to talk about it. This can prepare everyone's expectations for the funeral and help to avoid any unpleasant surprises on the occasion.

2. Send A Condolence Letter

If you want to go to the service but aren't sure how you'll be welcomed, think about how your presence will affect the family and those closest to the person who died. If you and your family have mutual acquaintances, you might want to reach out to them to obtain their perspectives on how your presence will affect them. If you think your attendance may upset the family but still want to show your condolences, you could skip the service and instead write a letter to the family expressing your condolences. Let them know why you stayed away in the letter.

3. Remember To Respect Everyone

If you eventually decide to attend the funeral or memorial service, you should remember to respect the people you meet there. Whether you agree with a family member's conduct or not, they are also grieving. Everyone is entitled to their moment and method of grieving. You may disagree with their choices or attitudes, but now is not the time to say so.

Validate the pain of others. Always keep in mind that you're all in this together. A funeral is a very emotional occasion. If fights or heated arguments emerge, family members will likely remember them for a long time. So don't be the center of attention. You'll be able to withdraw from your family and grieve in peace once the funeral is completed. So just ignore their bad attitude for a while. You wouldn't be there for long anyway.

■ When To Avoid Family Gatherings

If your family has physically or emotionally harmed you in the past, it's okay to say **NO** to family gatherings. As a result, you may be able to avoid becoming involved in an unpleasant situation. If you choose to skip a family gathering, be aware that you may experience great guilt and humiliation. This is very normal and will take some time to get used to.

You are better off staying in the peace and quiet of your room. Better off munching on a piece of the chicken pie and sipping your favorite juice than with family members that would rob you of your peace. Put yourself first. I promise you that you aren't missing out on any fun. You'd most likely not be happy if you were there.

You can also decide to skip family gatherings if you are:

Not Closely Related To The Celebrant Of The Event

You can decide to skip an event if you do not have a very close relationship with the major celebrant of the event. Even if they've never harmed you emotionally or physically, you might have an uneasy or distant connection with your family. These events can be stressful, and you may feel uncomfortable going.

If it becomes too much for you to take, you can make a quick appearance before leaving. For example, you may tell them that you're sick and you need to go.

Get Overwhelmed Easily or Are Introverted

You're not alone if you find family gatherings overwhelming. Having everyone in the same place for so long might be exhausting. You can make up a list of reasons why you won't be able to attend. I won't judge you for this; I do it a lot too.

Dislike Dealing With Questions and Gossips

One inevitable thing in family gatherings is the chatter, gossip, and weird questions you'll face. If you can't deal with all of these, you could decide to skip the event. You may feel bad about your decision not to attend family occasions, especially if family members begin to question you or gossip about why you didn't attend. Remember that you have the right to make the best decision for yourself, and no one can take that away from you.

You can stop the chatter and be open about your reasons for staying out of family gatherings. However, this technique may cause some people to feel offended.

You can shift the blame to yourself if you can't be open about your reasons. For example, say that large parties overwhelm you and cause anxiety and that you prefer smaller groups or one-on-one meetings.

Say it directly. You can tell your family in a clear and simple manner that you will no longer be attending family functions. You don't have to go into depth about why especially if the person you're speaking with does not know they are toxic. Consider how your family may react before speaking with them. Also, practice how you can stay calm and unwavering even if the situation turns heated. It would be best to consider whether you'll inform them in person, over the phone, or by text. Choose the safest option and go with your instincts.

You owe no one an explanation, and it's perfectly fine if you don't want to say anything and choose not to show up. Detaching yourself from toxic people can be quite tough, but as an adult who should know what's good for you, you have the right to choose what's good for you, including avoiding toxic family members.

Chapter 7: Keep Your Head Into Place In A Toxic Environment

" Just because they are your family doesn't mean that they know what's best for you or your life."

 Samuel Zulu

After the toxicity I got from my family members, it became obvious that I needed to work on myself. Not because I was offending them, but because I needed to get things right with them. I was mentally, emotionally, and psychologically affected. I could not go a day without having negative thoughts about my family members. I developed intense feelings of anger, and I wasn't at peace with them. This slowed down my healing process.

The fact that I was holding on to the toxicity I got and refused to let go affected me greatly. It didn't make my journey any faster. I figured that I needed to work on myself and my mind. And so, I began to let go of the hurt and hate. It was hard to do it because my family refused to accept that they were toxic. But I had to let it go. That was the only way if I wanted to move on.

I felt heavy loads drop off my mind as I progressed in my journey. I loved that feeling of freedom; it felt good. Empathy and forgiveness are what helped me move on quickly. It's difficult, but don't hold grudges against those who have wronged you, and don't condemn them either.

■ What Is A Toxic Environment?

Let me start by telling you how I discovered that I grew up in a toxic family. That would be more relatable and help you understand better. As a child, I absorbed all that was thrown at me by my family because I had no idea of what was right or wrong. This is actually how all children are. Their definition of right or wrong comes from what happens in their environment. So the insults from my parents and the unhealthy competition between my brother and me seemed normal because that was what I grew up facing.

The problem started when I was grown enough to discover myself well. I read books, made inquiries, learned and unlearned a lot of things. I learned that a toxic environment leaves you feeling unsafe, your palms begin to sweat, your headaches, your teeth clench, you get nervous, and you might even get the sudden urge to pee. If you experience all these, you're in a toxic environment.

A toxic environment will make you feel physically, mentally, and emotionally unsafe. It is a place where you feel unloved and unwanted. Most times, you'll feel drained and exhausted while you are there. The environment leaves a negative feeling in you, making communication with people extremely difficult.

A toxic environment is any space detrimental to your health, happiness, and well-being. For example, you may be in a toxic environment if you are surrounded by people who make you feel small and insecure. Maybe you go to work, and your boss verbally abuses you, or perhaps you have a sibling manipulating you in a way that crumbles your self-esteem. There's a possibility that you're creating a toxic environment for yourself. For example, when you don't keep your space tidy, or don't take care of yourself by watching a movie or reading a book once in a while.

When you dread the amount of time you have to spend in a particular place or with a particular set of people, that environment is toxic to you. In a toxic environment, there are usually heated arguments, angry outbursts, physical fights, use of cuss words, invasion of privacy, controlling behavior, constant criticism or ignorance of your feelings, and much more.

■ Why Are Toxic Environments Detrimental?

The mind is the basic essence of our being. It controls everything we do or say. It controls how we act and react. It is also in charge of our beliefs, experiences, and decisions after going through those experiences. The major reason toxic environments harm people is that they damage the mind. Toxic environments damage the mind in ways that are difficult to repair.

The worst kinds of pain are those that cannot be seen but felt. They cannot be cured by herbs or medicine. Damage to the mind is damage to the whole being. Once a person's mind is damaged, the entirety of the person is, in turn, damaged.

When you are displeased or hurt by your surroundings and the attitudes of the people around you, it is near impossible to be happy and healthy. Your mood and energy levels may suffer, and you may develop heart problems or other serious ailments. A toxic environment causes depression and anxiety.

Toxic environments are also detrimental because they can affect your personal and intimate relationships. For example, women constantly exposed to toxic environments may be unable to feel arousal. Toxicity can impact every aspect of your life, including your bedroom.

Are You A Toxic Person? How To Stop It?

As hard as it is, you might be the toxic one. We are quick to judge others without considering whether we are at fault. I'll tell you some indicators that you are a toxic person.

- ○ When a person feels unloved after spending time with you, there's a good chance you've acted toxically toward them. You might not know how they feel, but if you notice their body language becoming negative, they're probably in a bad mood because you've been toxic to them.

- ○ The fact that others avoid interacting with you is perhaps the clearest indication that you are toxic. You are most likely toxic if your friends seem to have other plans or make excuses for not meeting up with you. Another sign is if people frequently leave your life as soon as they enter it.

- ○ You are extremely critical of others and believe you are superior to them. You have difficulty accepting other people as they are and will frequently criticize or judge them for what you perceive to be their flaws. You dismiss their choices and make fun of their accomplishments.

- You are tyrannical and highly manipulative. You love to have your way no matter what it takes. You boss people around and use various forms of emotional blackmail. You can be extremely blunt and rude. You also pretend to be upset and use tears to guilt people into doing what you want.

- Because you can't do anything wrong, you immediately look for someone else to blame when something goes wrong in your life. Nothing bad is ever your fault. It is the result of other people's mistakes.

- While good friends can put up with a little friendly banter, it becomes toxic when you make it a habit to belittle people in front of a group of others constantly. For example, if your friendly 'banter' is a personal attack on an innocent person, that person will feel terrible about themselves, which is the defining characteristic of a toxic relationship.

○ When something goes well for someone else, or they succeed at a goal they set for themselves, you do not rejoice with them. You do not express your congratulations or express your joy for them. You could even dismiss their victory as insignificant or claim they were just lucky somehow. You also try to beat their achievements to make what they accomplished appear insignificant.

○ You do not keep secrets. Nobody wants to speak to you because you don't keep other people's secrets. Instead, you casually reveal these secrets when you believe they can be used to your advantage to gain the favor of third parties.

○ You try to play the victim. You believe that you suffer more than others, that your situation is more difficult. And you aren't afraid to tell or show others this is the case. You're always complaining about how other people treat you. You never stop to appreciate everything you have to be thankful for. This victim mentality makes you defensive; it causes you to lash out at the world and can lead you to mistreat yourself to show others how difficult things are for you.

These are some indicators that you are a toxic person and need to work on yourself. You can stop the toxicity by making conscious changes and adjustments to yourself. Acknowledging that you exhibit toxic behaviors sometimes is the first step to take to become a better person. This is because most toxic people refuse to accept that they have some toxic traits, making it harder for them to become better people. Since you acknowledge that you may have some toxic traits, the following steps aim to help you stop being the problem.

Identify Your Toxic Behaviors

It is easier to eliminate certain behaviors when you know exactly what you are dealing with and how intense it is. The approach to stopping playing the victim is different from the approach you will use to stop making snide remarks about people. This is why you need to identify which behavior you want to eliminate.

Make Conscious and Consistent Effort

Getting rid of your toxic behavior does not happen in just a day. It takes intentionality and conscious effort to stop. You might fail a few times, but that should not stop your drive to change. If you find yourself making belittling comments about someone, you can immediately say sorry and sincerely apologize for doing that. You would also need to be open to criticism. Listen to what people constantly complain about. Weigh it and make amends to correct it.

Seek Professional Help

Depending on the intensity and frequency at which you exhibit the already identified toxic behaviors, you might need professional help. Of course, you can change on your own, but you will most likely find that changing is easier and faster if you seek the help of a qualified therapist.

They'll be able to get to the bottom of your behavior and unravel the past in a method that's both safe and useful for dealing with it. They'll also assist you in developing healthier methods of interacting with and treating others.

Online counseling is more convenient than in-person therapy and can be significantly less expensive. In addition, you will receive the same high-quality care from fully qualified specialists. You can find excellent professionals that perform online in the link at the end of chapter 10.

■ 5 Tips to Keep Your Peace in a Toxic Environment

When you're in a toxic environment, keeping your cool can prove to be difficult. So I will share ten tips that would help you keep calm despite all the toxic activities around you.

Pay Attention To Body Signals

You have to notice the slightest changes that your body makes when you are in a toxic place. It might be your body telling you that you need space. For example, when your head starts to ache, your stomach starts to rumble, and your feet start to quiver. These are all signs that you need to take note of. Once you notice these signs, leave the environment for a while. Have a cup of water, and you'll be back to your cool self.

Keep Yourself Busy Doing What You Love

You can keep calm in a toxic environment by doing something you love. For example, if having a conversation with the people around you will make you feel uneasy, you can do something else. Play games, read a book, and spend time with pets. It will help you stay occupied and avoid toxicity.

Mind Your Business

Making it a duty to ignore any question or gesture that is not directed at you will help you maintain sanity in a toxic environment. You are avoiding a lot of trouble by minding your own business. You should only engage in conversations or reply to questions that are asked to you directly. Do not go into rooms you are not called into.

Know Thyself

Know what can calm you down in the case of a misunderstanding. You should have activities that can help you calm down. It could be breathing exercises or meditation. It could also be listening to music that helps you calm down. Just know yourself and do what works for you.

Be Compassionate

We all agree that toxic people could be a lot of trouble, but they are still human at the end of the day. Do not judge them; be compassionate. Recognize that everyone is going through a healing process from prior traumatic events or unresolved feelings. That's their procedure, and it's up to them to deal with it.

Toxic environments can be avoided in some situations. However, in situations where you cannot avoid toxic environments, you can use the tips above to cope while you are there. After you've exhausted your options, the only thing left is to take a step back and concentrate on your process. It's important that you cultivate this awareness in yourself to reach your higher self, a version of yourself who has mastered forgiveness, empathy, and maturity.

Chapter 8: You Don't Have To Be An Empath To Have Empathy

It takes empathy, patience, and forgiveness to overcome anger, hatred, and resentment."

Martin Luther King

Everything is extreme in a toxic environment! There are extreme outbursts of positive and negative emotions; yelling, sadness, or even anger is very profound in toxic environments. This makes people who grow up in environments like these extremely attuned to their moods and emotions. As a result, they might either become resistant to emotions or become extremely empathetic. In this chapter, we will discuss empathy and how it works.

■ What Is Empathy?

Empathy means understanding another person's feelings and emotions from their perspective rather than yours. It is not like sympathy, where you feel moved by another person's feelings but keep an emotional distance. Empathy is the ability to put yourself in another person's shoes and experience what they are experiencing. Empathy is when you witness someone suffering, and you can imagine yourself in their shoes and empathize with their situation. People who can empathize can comprehend what others are going through.

Empathy, when used as a tool, can be very beneficial. It will help you function well and relate with people effectively. Effective communication would also be easy when empathy is used correctly. Empathy itself is not a bad thing. It is a normal human emotion that anyone can feel. The problem starts when you become an extreme empath. Being an empath might be very detrimental to you, especially when you are around toxic family members. You begin to carry the feelings (whether positive or negative) of others and make them your own.

■ The Extreme Empath versus The Regular Empathetic Person

The difference between an empath and a regular person that uses empathy as a tool is very clear. The empathetic person can function maximally and relate well with others, while the empath takes things a little too personally. Being an extreme empath messes with your personality and emotions. This is because an empath absorbs other people's energy and feelings, while empathy helps you understand or have an idea of people's situations without absorbing the negative energy. If you can show empathy does not necessarily mean you are an empath. Similarly, you do not need to be an empath to show empathy.

An empath is a person who is very sensitive to the feelings and emotions of others. Their ability to understand what others feel extends beyond empathy to taking those feelings on. They can feel what another person is feeling on a strong emotional level. Even when they are fatigued, emotionally overwhelmed, and exhausted, empaths push themselves out of their comfort zone and start thinking, feeling, and doing for others.

Listening to the news or watching sad movies might be distressing for empaths. This is because they take on other people's pain and are too sensitive. Empaths easily become overwhelmed in crowded places too. For example, when I visited a friend who happened to be going back and forth with her son because he broke a glass cup. If I were an empath, I would get angry simply because my friend is angry. Instead, I have absorbed that angry energy and made it my own.

On the other hand, a regular person who effectively uses empathy as a tool will be able to feel the pain of others without absorbing the painful energy. This person can listen to someone, feel the person's pain, and proffer reasonable solutions where possible. It all comes down to listening and responding in a way that demonstrates that you understand your friend's point of view.

When you can use empathy as a tool effectively, you will be able to relate well with people around you.

You will not feel overwhelmed. You will understand and feel people's pain but not to the point where it harms your emotional well-being.

Let us use the scenario involving my friend, her son, and a broken cup I mentioned earlier. As someone that knows how to use empathy effectively, I would feel my friend's anger. But I would not just stop there. I would also communicate how I feel to her and proffer useful solutions to help fix the cup and calm her down.

■ 3 Types of Empathy

There are three ways that a person might experience empathy. They are:

Affective Empathy

This is the ability to understand and react accordingly to another person's emotions. It helps you understand and share another person's feelings and pains without absorbing the negative energy. This kind of empathy aids the development of emotional bonds with people. The emotional bond that this kind of empathy creates causes you to worry about the well-being of another person going through something you may or may not have experienced before.

I have a friend who lost his dog. He forgot to lock the dog's cage, and the dog wandered away. My friend called to rant to me and tell me about how bad he felt. He was not happy at all. Subconsciously, I began to reflect on how terrible I felt when my dog died. I remembered how I had spent the entire day crying. I felt like my most expensive toy was taken away from me. It helped me to understand how my friend felt too.

I was concerned about my friend because affective empathy helped me remember how I felt when I went through a similar situation. Affective empathy will enable you to not only understand but also share your friend's feelings. You strive to connect with a part of yourself that understands great sadness and emotional agony. For example, you might recall how it felt when you lost someone close to you or imagine how it would feel if you had not experienced that.

Somatic Empathy

This entails having a physical reaction to what another person is going through. Some people can sometimes physically feel what another person is going through. This is a result of somatic empathy.

I remember when my cousin visited. We talked a lot and had a nice time. I made a remark about how cute her son was. I noticed that she was smiling, and I subconsciously started smiling too. When you observe someone else crying or feeling sad, you might begin to manifest physical signs that show you are affected by what the person is going through.

Somatic empathy extends to physical experiences, which is why we grimace when someone else accidentally bumps their head on a wall. In this scenario, you'd dig within yourself to find a situation in which you were similarly affected. Because each person is unique, the situation does not have to be the same. What matters is that the emotions that arise from the scenario are the same.

When your friend is sad or has an upset stomach, you begin to cry or have a headache or maybe even an upset stomach too; it is somatic empathy

Cognitive Empathy

Understanding another person's emotional state and what they could be thinking in response to a situation is referred to as cognitive empathy. This is the ability to comprehend how another person feels and thinks. We become better communicators as a result of cognitive empathy. It allows us to communicate information in the most effective way possible to the other person. This is connected to the theory of mind, or thinking about what other people think.

Let us imagine that your friend lost a sibling. Your friend is obviously going through a tough time. Cognitive empathy can help you to understand what your friend is going through. You try to imagine how close they are to the deceased. Aside from the pain of losing a sibling, you will try to imagine how their lives will change.

■ Signs Of Empathy

You might be confused as to whether you are an empath or not. The examples below are key indicators that you are an empath.

- You have a knack for paying attention to what others have to say.
- People frequently confide in you about their problems.
- You have a keen sense of how other people are feeling.
- You frequently consider how other people are feeling.
- Others come to you for guidance and advice.
- Tragic circumstances frequently overwhelm you.
- You make an effort to assist others who are in need.

- You have a good sense of when someone is not being truthful.
- In social gatherings, you may feel easily fatigued or overwhelmed.
- You genuinely care about other people.
- You have a hard time setting boundaries in your relationships with others.
- Too much familiarity or connection with someone can be emotionally draining.
- You can deduce how the other person is feeling at the moment by observing tiny cues such as facial expressions and nonverbal gestures.
- You're always willing to listen.
- You are a peacemaker who despises strife and fights.
- You effortlessly absorb other people's emotional responses and adopt them as your own, to the point where you get emotionally drained.
- You may feel overburdened due to being available to others, and you may need to

remove yourself from people to unwind and recuperate.

■ Tips For Practicing Empathy

Empathy is a part of our everyday life as humans. This is why practicing empathy effectively in our everyday life is a skill that everyone must learn. Fortunately, it is a skill that can be learned and improved on. Here are a few things you can do to improve your empathy skills:

Active Listening: Practice Paying Attention To Others Without Interrupting Them

Interrupting someone while speaking implies that you do not value what they are saying. It implies that what you have to say is more significant than what others have to say. This is why it is important to pay attention and refrain from interrupting.

Not only should you listen, but you should also speak up. Empathy is about showing oneself to others and feeling empathy for others. Building a good and empathic relationship with someone else requires trusting them with your honest thoughts and feelings. Empathy is a two-way street. It has the potential to go both ways. So, while you listen, make sure to share your experiences too.

Pay Attention To Nonverbal Messages

Some people show their discomfort using body language. Paying attention to non-verbal messages is very important. This is because some people might have difficulty communicating their problems verbally. Taking note of body language shows that you are concerned about the individual.

Understand Others' Perspectives

Even if you disagree with someone, try to understand their perspective. People believe that because someone disagrees with them or lives a different lifestyle than them, that person is undeserving of empathy. When empathy appears difficult, it is important to use your imagination and try to understand the other person's point of view.

Ask Questions

To discover more about people and their life, ask them questions. Empathetic people are curious about individuals around them. They might discuss with someone they don't know or study others with curiosity. They are individuals who have maintained the natural curiosity that we all have as children. Curiosity allows us to empathize by exposing us to other worldviews, cultures, and people we might not otherwise encounter.

Try To Picture Yourself In Someone Else's Shoes

Imagine that you were in the position someone else is in. How would you react? What would you need? Putting yourself in someone else's situation would help you feel empathy for the person. You can now decide to help out in your own way. This could be paying a visit to an orphanage or bringing inmates a meal. Incorporating yourself into the lives and experiences of others is a fantastic approach to improving your empathy.

■   Feelings That May Accompany Empathy

Feelings that might accompany empathy include guilt, anger, grudges, insecurity, and criticism. I will explain them below and mention how you can cope with them.

■ Guilt

A guilt complex is characterized by a continuous sense that you have done or will do something wrong. Even if you haven't done anything wrong, guilt will make you believe you have. It will make you exaggerate your own contribution to a situation.

A guilt complex can severely affect a person's physical and mental health. After a while, people with a guilt complex may start to harbor a sense of inadequacy that makes it hard to set goals and achieve them. Guilt is so terrible that it makes its victims feel they are incapable of moving on from their mistakes. It begins to make them engage in weird acts to punish themselves for their wrongdoings.

Replacing guilty thoughts with more positive ones will help you get over your feeling of guilt. Depending on the severity of your guilt, you may need medication to cope with it. The medication that your doctor would recommend is mostly antidepressants or anti-anxiety drugs. They would help you manage your symptoms. Your doctor might also recommend psychotherapy.

■ Grudge

Having and maintaining a feeling of rage or resentment towards someone for something you believe they committed against you is known as holding a grudge. When you hold a grudge, you are harboring anger, resentment, or other bad feelings after someone has wronged you. Usually, it's in response to something that has already happened, but a grudge can also arise from simply suspecting that someone is against you or intends to hurt you.

You may recall several previous unpleasant deeds and relive those memories whenever you think about or contact that person. Most people carry a grudge on purpose, but some may not even be aware that they are doing it. The carrier will try to avoid having anything to do with the person he's carrying the grudge against. And in most cases, most grudges are one-sided. Just one party is aware and has decided not to communicate with the other person. Some people may refer to this as malice. However, they both mean the same.

Are you experiencing this and need a solution? Maybe this could help. Have you tried calling the person and expressing your feelings? This is a very effective way to deal with such. When some people don't say certain things, they tend to bottle and keep it within, and they would continue to hold on to it. But if you call the person, tell the person how you feel, and there's a resolution, you'll see no need to hold grudges against such persons. Sometimes, some people do certain things that make the other party angry, and they are not even aware. This is where communication comes in. Both parties are happy, and they both reconcile and move on peacefully.

■ Anger

It's natural for us to get angry from time to time. Anger is a healthy and natural emotion. It isn't always a 'bad' emotion; in fact, it can be beneficial at times. Anger only becomes an issue when it spirals out of control and causes harm to you or others. Being constructive with your anger will go a long way in helping you not to cause harm when angry.

To achieve this, try to know your triggers and avoid them. As humans, we all have things that trigger our anger. It is one thing to know these things, and it is another thing to avoid them consciously. This is a good way of curbing and managing anger when it sets in. Once you notice the anger, you can walk away from whatever or just choose to ignore it. Many people get very angry because they choose to be the reactive type. If you react to almost everything, then the tendency to get angry is very high.

To overcome this feeling, you can try to engage yourself in activities that make you happy. It could be anything. Once you're in the process of making yourself happy, then you're on your way to getting less angry. If the matter gets out of hand, you need to seek psychotherapy. This is an effective way of treating anger.

■ Insecurity

Insecurity is characterized by a sense of inadequacy, not being good enough, and apprehension. It causes you to be worried about your goals, relationships, and ability to deal with specific events. It could also be caused by a state of general instability in your life. People subjected to unpredictably disruptive events in their daily lives are more likely to feel apprehensive about their everyday resources and routines. Sometimes, your environment and people around you could also facilitate that feeling of security. For example, you see many of your peers doing well, and that feeling just comes and makes you feel you're not doing enough. Nobody is immune to this feeling as it can happen to just anyone.

To be a step ahead, you need to watch the people you keep close and move with. If they are not people that make you feel lesser than you are, then your problem is half solved because the people you are close to having some influence on you and the way you think too. If you have the opposite around you, then the tendency to feel insecure is very high.

Another thing to do to fight this feeling of insecurity is to celebrate your small wins. You don't need to hit a mega jackpot before you acknowledge yourself. No matter how little your achievements are, try to applaud yourself and celebrate them. This will instill a vibe of optimism and more positivity in you.

You also need to be proud of whatever you have or do. This will go a long way because people will always be entitled to their opinions. But if you're very proud of yourself, any third party's opinion will matter less to you because you already have that inner self-validation within you.

■ Coping With Criticism Appropriately

When relating with toxic people, it might seem like you are walking on eggs, trying not to break anyone. Toxic people are very quick to take offense; this is probably why people keep their distance. They might make you feel bad for trying to correct or advise them. They may even make it feel like you are a toxic person, making you unsure of yourself and where you stand. However, you should not be upset or frightened.

A toxic person is fighting an internal battle. What they do to you or people around them reveals a lot more about them than the act itself. This is why many people who relate to toxic people prefer not to have anything serious to do with them to avoid any troubles or problems. Toxic people are everywhere humans are. In fact, every human should have at least one toxic individual they know. That's to show you how widespread they are. Knowing that it is inevitable to avoid them totally, you can still try to relate with them in certain manners that may not trigger them.

When you want to criticize, try to be constructive with your criticism as much as possible. You praise first, then constructively state the shortcomings, then you praise again. This is a strategy that has worked over time. As much as you try to avoid them, there's still room for a balance.

Another thing to avoid is the words you use when communicating with them. Again, using more polite words will do a lot to help them cope with this. But if you use abusive or insulting words, you've successfully triggered that side of them you are avoiding.

Chapter 9: The Differences Between a Narcissist vs. Toxic vs. Flawed Person

Refuse to inherit dysfunction. Learn new ways of living instead of repeating what you lived through."

Thema Davis

The good sides of a person are always there for us to see. We only need to learn to recognize people's best qualities and, more importantly, let them know by telling them and complimenting them so that they know their worth. Despite treating family members, coworkers, and friends horribly, some people's negative attitudes do not define who they are.

Everyone has positive talents. It will make a difference when you start complimenting or commenting on the great qualities of toxic relatives. This warms their heart and makes them believe they can improve on themselves. The good feeling that comes with being praised because they were kind to others will encourage them to be nicer and take better care of others.

Do not be quick to judge others. You may be tempted to label someone toxic, narcissistic or flawed because of how they behave. I'm afraid that's not that quick to assimilate. Only a qualified professional should do that. They have the knowledge, the precision, and experience to diagnose a patient.

Earlier, I discussed my fight with my brother and how we drifted apart. But, of course, I still miss him, despite his terrible behavior. Even with his toxicity, he still has his amazing sides.

Everyone has a good side. As much as we may believe that our toxic family members are terrible people, they still have a piece of goodness in them. I still don't talk to my brother as much as I would want to, but I miss that good part of him. I miss the other good conversations we can have, but I had to do what was best for me.

This chapter will clarify the traits of different personalities of people.

■ Narcissist Behavior

A healthy sense of self can be beneficial. For example, some experts feel that people with high self-perceptions are mentally tougher and less prone to depression. On the other hand, narcissism is characterized by an exaggerated feeling of self-importance, a lack of empathy for others, and a strong desire for constant attention.

Narcissism is a form of severe self-indulgence that makes people overlook the needs of everyone else around them. While everyone exhibits narcissistic behavior occasionally, real narcissists constantly ignore others and their feelings. They also have no understanding of the impact their actions have on others. The ego of a narcissist can be extremely fragile, relying on external affirmation or self-deception. They will have unrealistic ideas about themselves.

Narcissists think they're brighter, more gorgeous, and more successful than everyone around them. So they tear others down and take over any conversation or circumstance to make themselves feel better or superior. Feeling "less than flawless" is extremely unpleasant for a narcissist, and they will do anything to avoid it.

Main Characteristics of a Narcissist

- Lack of empathy.

- Exaggerated sense of self-importance.

- The strong desire for undivided attention and adoration.

- Relationships that are always in a state of flux, never stagnant in inertia.

○ Fantasy of limitless power, brilliance, beauty, or love.

○ The notion that only other special or high-status people should associate with them.

○ A constant need to be recognized and praised.

○ Sense of entitlement.

○ Interpersonal exploitation (they view the people in their lives as objects—there to serve their needs) without guilt or shame.

Causes of Narcissistic Behavior

Studies suggest that narcissism is caused by a malfunction in a child's relationships in his formative years. For example, a person who experienced maltreatment or neglect, excessive parental attention and control, and unreasonable expectations from parents will likely end up a narcissist.

Covert And Overt Narcissist

Covert narcissism is defined by the same characteristics as overt narcissism but in a more subtle, less visible manner. The approach of a covert narcissist is overtly self-effacing or aloof, but the end aims are the same. Covert narcissists are typically quiet, overly sensitive to people's perceptions, and very envious. They frequently believe that their suffering is greater than everyone.

■ Toxic Behavior

It may not easy to define someone toxic so quickly, but it is very easy to spot a toxic behavior. You will feel it right away. Toxic attitudes are very draining. We all judge people once in a while, but a toxic person always judges people. Toxic people are unable to see the positive aspects of life. They will hardly find delight in positivity. Being with someone like this makes it difficult to relax and enjoy yourself.

Toxic people are mainly concerned about themselves. They don't care about how their actions affect others and believe they are superior to others. Self-centered people are focused on achieving what they want and are unwilling to compromise or consider the opinion of others. They can be master manipulators who frequently twist your words or make you feel bad to get what they want.

■ Flawed Person

The words *'narcissist'* and *'toxic'* are thrown around so freely these days. I want you to know that no one is completely perfect; I am not perfect, and neither are you. A person with a flaw may not necessarily be toxic.

A flawed person has specific and isolated imperfections in their character and is willing to change. A flawed person recognizes that they may not be right and are eager to improve if they are found to be wrong, even if they take a while to realize it.

I remember how my grandfather fussed over things like someone breaking a glass, staining the house's white walls by accident, laying dirty feet on the sofa, or keeping the house disorganized. He continues to treat the rest of the family in that manner, emphasizing his importance, enforcing rules, and treating his home with reverence; in the manner in which he had been brought up. To me, that's fine; he's who he is, and we can't change him. But we can mold ourselves by extracting what we need to absorb from him and letting go of what we don't want to retain in our lives.

He had certain defects in his personality and outlook on life, considering that he comes from a much different generation in 1940. When certain habits start looking worrying and make you feel scared and upset, you can look further to determine if it is toxicity or narcissism. Also, we need to understand that we are humans; we fail, have desires, have needs, feel, try new things, strive, and succeed. It's in our nature. So we are not perfect; we are all flawed in one way or the other. That's why seeking help from professional therapists is so important, so we can separate these things before we go out there labeling our relatives, or any other people.

■ 28 Examples of a Flawed Person

Extreme Jealous Person

An extremely jealous person may not appear to be jealous. They may look pleasant on the outside, but they are envious on the inside. They may never show hate, hostility, or harbor a grudge against somebody, but their actions betray them in subtle ways. Extreme jealousy can be noticed in subtle reactions. For example, a jealous person will fake a smile for you in social gatherings. They will fake being friendly with you, but when you're not there, they will criticize you, saying unpleasant things about you.

Greedy

Greedy people are the first to beg for more but the last to put in the effort needed to earn the benefits.

They believe they are entitled to the finest things, even if they come at a high price. Greedy people grab things that aren't theirs, even if it means putting their friends or people around them in danger.

They lie to cheat others. They believe others aren't intelligent enough to take advantage of the situation, so they don't deserve them.

Bad-tempered / Temperamental

People with terrible tempers will become enraged because of little things. They will always have an excuse when you try to talk to them about their anger. It's never their fault if they're irritated. It is someone or something that made them be that way. They will never let a disagreement go. If you try to have a rational conversation with them, it will result in a fight. And if they do not agree with something you do, they will never let it go, even if you are right.

Temperamental people have a great need to be right all the time and become enraged when they aren't.

Timid

Timid people are shy, apprehensive, and lack boldness and self-confidence. They are usually hesitant to try new activities or interact with new individuals. A timid person avoids social gatherings and conversations.

Although most timid people are introverts, not all introverts are timid. They lack confidence in their physical appearance and intellect, so they find it difficult to maintain a conversation.

Troublemaker

They are good at starting fights and arguments where it is not necessary. They are too dramatic and make a big deal out of trivial matters. They publicly harass people around them to disrupt their work and gain attention. It is easy to recognize them. Troublemakers have a knack for causing chaos.

Idealist

Idealists tend to be introverted and driven by high values. Idealists value personal feelings above all else, and their actions are affected by these feelings rather than logical reasoning. Idealists prefer to keep their choices open while making decisions. They usually put off making key decisions in case the circumstance may change. Their decisions are made based on personal ideals rather than logic. They can be extremely idealistic and take everything personally.

Impatient

Impatient people want things done immediately and may become frustrated if things take time. They put pressure on people to complete tasks in their preferred manner. As a result, they frequently act on the spur of the moment without taking the required precautions.

They may become irritated by delays, particularly if they believe they are unnecessary. They make rash decisions based on incomplete knowledge.

Immature

Emotionally immature people do not meet society's social behavior expectations for their age group. They struggle to relate with others because they lack specific emotional and social abilities. They are very impulsive. They speak inappropriately or touch things they shouldn't touch. They say things without considering how they would affect others. Emotionally immature people don't have control over their urges. They behave in erratic or antisocial ways. They may not behave in a harmful manner, but they may interrupt conversations or make inappropriate jokes to gain people's attention.

Emotionally immature people can't plan for the future. They avoid responsibility and refuse to take on important things such as being committed in relationships, careers, or finances.

Soft-hearted

A soft-hearted person is extremely emotional. They may be compassionate and good, yet they can get more angry, hurt, irritated, or frustrated than others. They do not have a mind of their own because they are too empathetic. They act based on impulse. Their actions are guided by their emotions. When soft-hearted people are angry, it's extreme, and it's difficult to calm them down. Their words and actions change with their emotions.

Self-righteous

Self-righteous people are frequently intolerant of the viewpoints and behaviors of others. They believe everything they do is right, acting like they are perfect. They pass the blame to others even when they are wrong. Self-righteous people live on attention.

Selfish

A selfish person only looks out for themselves. They are never concerned about the well-being of others. As long as they are okay, every other person doesn't matter. Promises made by a selfish person are not kept. They merely make false promises to earn approval from people. They love to brag; they're arrogant and self-centered.

They want all the attention to be on them when outside. Selfish people are not interested in making mental or emotional connections with others. They can't create a solid bond unless they see a benefit in it. All they care about is what they can get from people.

Seducer

A seducer will lure you into doing something bad and make it seem like you did it without their influence. Seducers lure people and make them do things they normally would not do. They are good at starting trouble and getting away with it. Seducers love to gaslight others. They lead people on and make them unsure of what they want.

Once a seducer successfully lures you, they will leave you alone to bear the repercussions of what they made you do. They drag people into a ditch, fight, or messy situation and leave them to bear the consequences alone.

Sarcastic

Sarcastic people crack jokes that belittle people. Sarcasm is more than a sense of humor. It's making comments to hurt someone's feelings or mock someone. Sarcastic people can be manipulative. When it comes to relationships, sarcastic people flaunt their cleverness at the expense of others.

Skeptic

People who are skeptics are always in doubt. They may interrogate you and make you feel as if you are lying when you say something. They feel that there must be a deeper or underlying meaning to everything. They will look for stories behind everything you say to figure out what's happening.

They ask many questions and follow up on answers they don't believe.

Audacious

They are bold and very rude. They challenge anyone, anywhere. They believe they need to know more than they already do, so they never miss a chance to challenge or dare people. They love to argue to prove their point. They can be very noisy too.

Rigorous

These individuals have powerful personalities. A rigorous individual encourages others to take action. As a result, many people with this personality are self-sufficient. Because of their strong personality, they may unknowingly impose their thoughts or ideas on others. They might also be pompous and difficult to approach.

Rebellious

A rebellious person enjoys defying authority and occasionally breaking the rules. They are continually looking for methods to stand out.

Others may find them unapproachable. They enjoy taking the lead. People that are rebellious question everything. They could also look disorganized. They are very similar to troublemakers.

Pride

Even if they are wrong, proud individuals will not accept or apologize for their faults. They love to be the focus of attention at all times. They are self-obsessed with their physical appearance. They dislike hanging out with "regular" or unpopular people. They feel they know everything and are incapable of being taught. They don't pay attention to what others have to say. They believe they are too important to be bothered with trivial matters.

Practical

A practical person lacks empathy. They feel that everything can and should be solved with logic. They might be insensitive to the feelings and emotions of people around them. They have a no-nonsense approach to life.

They might be very rigid in their beliefs and actions. They do not have time for drama and move on from problems quickly.

Perfectionist

A perfectionist is quick to judge those who make mistakes. They believe the second place is just another way of saying "first loser." Perfectionists are more concerned with what others have to say about them. They are prone to reacting negatively to constructive criticism. They also procrastinate a lot. Fear of failing is one of the most damaging features of maladaptive perfectionism. This fear manifests as procrastination and other avoidance behaviors.

Pessimist

A pessimist is one who doesn't see the good in any situation. They have reasons why something bad will happen. They are arrogant and can be very rude. They have lower risk tolerance. They don't pursue their goals since they believe they will likely fail. They are continuously thinking about what could go wrong in a situation. Almost every time, they believe the risks outweigh the benefits.

Oppressor

The oppressor forces their beliefs on everyone around them. They believe that things should be done their way. They order people around when they are placed in high positions. Intimidating words, insults, threats, and physical violence are used by oppressors. They use harsh and unpleasant methods to exercise authority or dominance over others. The oppressors are blind to the violent and unfair actions that keep them in power, so they simply use more force against anyone who dares to oppose them. Oppressors treat others in a repressive manner. A desire for power and dominance drives them.

Obsessive

An obsessive person wants to know and be in charge of everything. Perfectionism and thoroughness are two characteristics that best describe an obsessional personality. People with this personality type pay close attention to every detail in their environment and themselves.

Individuals with this personality trait may spend so much of their time doing chores, preparing schedules, and making lists of things to do that the main goal of the activity is overlooked. The individual feels responsible for everything that needs to be done. Obsessive people feel that everything must be perfect and that it is their obligation to ensure it is.

Nosey

These people are very tricky. They want to be in everyone's business, even if it has nothing to do with them. Nosy persons are overly concerned with what other people are doing and tend to breach others' privacy. Nosy people are snoopy and intrusive. They believe that because you have a relationship with them, they have the right to know everything about you. As a result, they don't know how to interact with other people.

Lazy

Lazy people are grumpy. They constantly have an excuse for why they can't complete a task. Instead of working, they delegate their responsibilities to others. They put off doing specific activities until the very last minute, driving themselves to rush to complete them despite having plenty of time beforehand. They are chronic procrastinators with terrible time management skills. They never engage in any physical activity.

Indifferent

They don't care about anything and show apathy towards everything. They do not want to be on any side or participate in anything. They are just there, and they show an indifferent attitude. They don't argue, communicate, or air their opinions in gatherings; they don't reciprocate good deeds. Most times, they are lonely because people do not want to have anything to do with them, and they're also not lovable. They're bad communicators and can't make decisions.

Alcoholic

Alcohol is one of the most addictive substances humans take. And when this addiction sets in, it affects the taker's personality. One top trait of alcoholic people is low self-esteem. They often feel lesser than themselves and feel inferior to others. Another attribute alcoholics exhibit is anxiety. There is this fear that comes with everything they want to do. And this anxiety can lead to temper problems. They tend to get angry at little things when they've taken the alcohol; from here, frustration sets in. So being an alcoholic has a whole lot of negatives attached to it.

Addiction

Addiction is a result of the persistent intake or use of certain substances. Once the system has acclimatized to the use of these substances, the individual begins to find it difficult to stop the use of substances. In addition, an addict will most likely suffer from mental instability. When drugs are abused, they have a lot of negative impacts on the users. Addicts are glued to the behaviors or things they're addicted to. They usually don't mind whatever they have to do to get these things. All that matters to them is to get them.

These flaws are specific, and they can occur singly in individuals. A person isn't automatically a narcissist. Their flaw has nothing to do with narcissism. People can have one or more of these flaws. So instead of using the word *'toxic'* or *'narcissist,'* you can point out the specific flaw that the person exhibits. Say "he's indifferent" or "she's nosey."

Chapter 10: The True Healing - Keep A Room For Better Days With Recovery and Reconciliation

If it's hurting you more than it's healing you, love yourself enough to let it go."

Sherrie Campbell

Family means different things to different people. However, as many suggest, it's not just a simple concept. On the contrary, family is a complex concept that a simple definition won't be enough since the experiences of one person could be different from the next person.

Like it was once said here: to some people, family is a special, genetic, or unique bond between people. For some others, it's more than just a bond. To them, family is the only place where they feel secure and completely relaxed; it is where their **"HOME"** is.

If you're part of the latter, family will mean the place where you get unconditional love, care, and support. If you're in a healthy family setting, you will look forward to returning home from wherever you are. You would be eager to return home to receive comfort, love, and attention from your family members.

On the other hand, home is different if you are in a toxic family system. Home might mean anxiety, fear, alienation, and lack of peace, warmth, comfort, unconditional love, and support. This type of home is where we least want to get back to.

This chapter focuses on recovering, reconciliation, and getting treatment to help you heal. To achieve all these, you need to let go of the things and people that hurt you. At the same time, you need to leave room for reconciliation since true healing requires you to forgive, make peace, and reconcile with the hurt.

Growing up in a toxic family might make the whole healing process seem almost impossible since you've always felt hollow, anxious, confused, and left alone to experience negative emotions. How can you possibly forgive, and everything will automatically be back to normal? True, it could be difficult but not impossible.

Living in a toxic family presents you with a unique form of *crazy* where you will feel like a sentient programmed to exist without experiencing the feelings you see others receive from their family and loved ones.

The dream of experiencing a healthy family would feel like a science-fiction movie where you can only dream about things but never experience them. You may have even felt envy and pain seeing other families' relationships. All these will build up negative emotions like hate, resentment, thoughts of self-harm, and many others.

But do we continue holding on to our toxic relationships or strive for healing and freedom? Remember, when you are free, you have the opportunity to experience what a healthy family feels like. This chapter will help point you in the right direction to help you heal and recover from toxic family members. We will discuss treatment and therapy to speed up the healing process and smooth transitioning from a toxic to a healthy family relationship.

But first, you need to accept your current conditions in the family and be willing to make eventual necessary changes.

■ Learning When To Walk Away

There are two folds to toxic relationship abuse. In the first layer, you'll face the poor treatment of close relatives and other family members, including your parents. The second layer of abuse is when you deny the poor treatment you receive, how they treat you, and how you've been harmed. Even with clear evidence of their behavior and poor treatment, you cling to the abuse, making you doubt your self-worth.

It worsens when you try to express your fears about life and love to others. You will appear needy, paranoid, and somewhat desperate. This is because emotional and psychological abuse are neither easy to explain nor equipped with descriptive indicators. Unfortunately, your family members capitalize on these facts to remain toxic without caring how you feel.

Because emotional abuse is difficult to put in words, without any provable, concrete terms, many sufferers begin to question their situation. I've been in a similar situation where I questioned if my abuse and neglect were real. At this moment, I was still making excuses to help justify why I felt the way I did and if I was being actually abused.

Unless you've had education concerning emotional abuse, you'll find it difficult to explain and come to terms with your situation fully. This allows our toxic family members to abuse you more emotionally. Moreover, toxic family members are good at concealing their abusive attacks, so when you talk subjectively about how they hurt you, they have a way of making themselves innocent victims of unfair accusations from an emotionally unstable person. This type of situation can be infuriating and compounds the hurt.

So how do we walk away from the hurt, abuse, and poor treatment?

Acceptance

What you're feeling is not just in your head; it is as real as it can get. If you're being talked down on and you find going home dreadful, then you're certainly not imaging the abuse and neglect. You have to accept that something is wrong to be able to progress further. You also need to understand that loving someone doesn't equate to having a good relationship with them. You can love someone from a distance.

An important part of your healing journey is acceptance. For example, accepting that you are being abused, that you need to let go of the people abusing you, that forgiveness doesn't always mean reconciliation, and that not reconciling with certain relatives even if you love them is normal.

Reconciliation

Some relationships are better off severed because they are toxic. They obstruct or destroy your healthy life and ability to function properly. Here, reconciling means you are setting up the stage for healing.

When you allow yourself to break free from toxic relatives, you give yourself the needed space to love them from a safe distance where they can't harm you, and in turn, you do not wish them any harm. You are not staying out of reach or running away. Instead, you're setting boundaries to the relationship because you're now more experienced to know that staying connected with them is unhealthy. But the main key to walking away is not to be far from them but to give them a chance for healing and reconciliation.

Cutting ties is basically getting rid of something. But that hurts and creates a hole in your heart that may keep grudges or negative emotional limitations. What I strongly suggest is: don't lose hope for those who hurt you. Keep respectful, and even from a distance, give it a chance to get in contact again. It doesn't need to break the boundaries you set. You can communicate with them and work on yourself, learning from the ways you felt and self-observing during the connection you had with them from time to time. This is a powerful thing, despite being uncomfortable.

■   Recovery

Now that you've come this far, restoring yourself and reclaiming your lost confidence, dignity, self-worth, and your sense of self-value, there are two important things you need to consider to make your recovery and healing complete. First, you need to consider a treatment plan, such as therapy and self-discovery.

Before I go deeper about treatments and therapies, let's first look at rediscovering yourself.

Rediscovering Yourself

Recovering doesn't mean bringing you back to your base and leaving things there. Instead, there's a need to rediscover yourself, define and decide what you want to do with your life. More so, it would help if you had a clear identity, confidence, and self-awareness, restored dignity and independence, were financially buoyant, and built a positive self-image to fit into society with no fear or shame of own self.

While recovering, it is also important to reflect on your past actions as a victim of a toxic family. That way, you can define a new you and not repeat your past mistakes. You need to ask yourself why you stayed. By asking yourself and accepting your answers, you can overcome the guilt remaining in you, either for walking away or staying for so long.

Some of the common reasons why people stay in a toxic and abusive relationship include:

Fear: In a toxic relationship, fear could mean fear of being physically abused, fear of meeting someone who will treat you even worse, or fear of being independent and surviving without the support of the toxic relative.

Love: It may be due to your love for that person, even if they are toxic. You might have invested much of your emotions and probably had good times, and you're hoping things will be alright.

Financial Dependency: Sometimes, the lack of finances and a means to earn can be a factor that binds you to a toxic situation.

Societal and Religious Expectations: Most times, keeping up a façade while giving people the impression that 'all is well' could keep you in a sad and toxic family. You could be avoiding societal shame or not want to disappoint God, your family, or your friends. Considering these factors, you choose to remain in a position where you are abused.

Emotional Dependency: It's not rare for people to depend on others before they can make any decisions for themselves. Some would be willing to remain in an abusive environment to have a companion, while others do so for the emotional support they get. Emotional dependency can even make you be in denial and question yourself if you were abused or you were thinking too much.

Family Stability: Many people are stuck in unhealthy relationships due to attachments such as their children or siblings. They make flawed sacrifices to keep their family together by remaining committed to having a stable family to avoid interruptions in the lives of the other family members. This way, they would never be able to decide to walk out of a toxic relationship.

There are so many people enduring toxic relationships for different reasons, but there are a few things they have in common, and that was something I also shared until I was able to get help. People who suffer from emotional abuse have in common: their attachments, inability to see the truth, inability to let go and walk away, and most importantly, their fear of dealing with reality.

Every time I did a therapy session, I was afraid of digging out all the dirt I had swept under the rug. I was really uncomfortable visiting those sad memories I thought I had buried and forgotten. But if you truly want to heal, you need to open up these covered wounds.

Just like a plaster that covers up a wound while protecting it from pain, you may hide your pain and emotions to feel comfortable, but you won't truly heal. To achieve true healing, you need to revisit, reconcile, and rediscover yourself. You need to take off that plaster and let your wound heal. Though it could hurt like crazy, what comes after the pain is lasting peace, the comfort, and peace of mind.

■ Treatment plans

At this point, you need to consider a good treatment plan. True healing also involves getting help for your mental state. Don't be afraid of therapy sessions with a professional therapist in Cognitive Behavioral Therapy (CBT). These experts are there to listen to you and guide you towards rediscovering yourself and fitting into society without fear or guilt. They help you heal from your hate and resentment.

■ Cognitive Behavioral Therapy (CBT)

Cognitive behavioral therapy (CBT) is a psycho-social treatment plan that helps you identify negative and unhealthy thoughts and behavior patterns. It is a form of talk therapy (psychotherapy) where you work with a therapist or psychotherapist, generally called mental health counselors, in controlled sessions.

CBT techniques have proven effective in identifying and exploring different ways our emotions and thoughts can affect our behaviors. By becoming aware of our negative or inaccurate thinking patterns, we can view challenging situations more clearly and effectively respond to them.

CBT techniques can be applied alone or in combination with other therapies in treating mental health issues, such as post-traumatic stress disorders (PTSD), depression, anxiety, substance misuse, substance use disorder, and eating disorders.

You should also note that not everyone who benefits from CBT suffers from a mental health condition. CBT can be used for several other conditions, including stress management and improving the general quality of life.

Core Concepts of CBT

CBT is mostly based on the notion that your thoughts, emotions, and actions (behaviors) are linked. This means that what you think and how you feel about a particular thing can affect your actions.

For example, let's assume you're under a lot of stress at home and work. Under such conditions, you might perceive or begin to view things differently and make decisions you wouldn't usually make. Meanwhile, CBT concepts believe that your thoughts and behavior patterns can be altered and changed using CBT techniques.

Popular CBT Techniques

Although CBT is not a one-size-fits-all and each session is different, some CBT techniques are popular among therapists, and these techniques are:

Decatastrophizing

Catastrophizing or catastrophic thinking is a form of cognitive thinking where we automatically see negative outcomes and believe the gravest possible consequences will occur no matter how impossible or unlikely such an outcome is.

Decatastrophizing exercises aim to help us whenever we begin to worry about something unnecessary repeatedly.

When you're caught in these unhealthy thinking patterns, decatastrophizing experts will recommend asking yourself questions such as:

- *What am I worried about?*
- *How possible will the things I worry about come true?*
- *If my worries ever come true, what's the worst possible outcome?*

- *What's the most likely thing to happen if my worry comes true?*

- *How would my life be affected if my worries came true?*

- *What are the chances I'll be okay?*

Asking yourself these questions could help you find simple answers and help you think rationally and calmly.

The ABC technique

This technique is designed to help you understand your activating events (A), your behaviors (B), and consequences (C). For example:

I. John was mean while talking to me (A)

II. I couldn't help myself from crying (B)

III. I've been avoiding him ever since because I got scared of him (C)

The ABC technique explores what happened (the events), your actions, how you acted, and what happened afterward.

These exercises aim to help us change our way of thinking, which will affect and change our behaviors.

These techniques have been used to examine and help criminals. *What made you steal? (A), You then committed a crime by stealing (B) and went to jail (C).*

The reason for confinement is to help offenders connect how they reacted to a situation with the consequences in hopes that the next time they experience A, they'll make different choices and react differently, which will affect the outcomes of B and C.

Keeping a journal

This technique involves writing and documenting the things that happen and how you feel about them. The aim is to help you better understand your emotions and thought processes.

As time passes, you can begin to self-identify common problems or challenges in your thinking. Then, you can discuss them with your counselor or therapist and work on finding solutions to manage them.

Psychoanalysis

Psychoanalysis is a set of psychological theories and therapeutic methods which are deeply rooted in the work and theories of Sigmund Freud. Today, psychoanalysis has become a valuable tool that many therapists on CBT use in their treatments. So, don't find it strange when you hear about psychoanalysis during your therapy session.

Theory of Mind

One of the main assumptions of psychoanalysis is based on the principle that all humans possess unconscious thoughts, desires, and memories.

Freud's Three Levels of Mind

Freud described the mind and separated it into three distinct levels, the **preconscious**, the **conscious**, and the **unconscious** mind, with each performing its own roles and functions.

The preconscious mind: This level consists of anything that could be brought into the conscious mind.

The conscious mind: This level of the mind holds all your thoughts, feelings, memories, and wishes that you are aware of at that particular moment. This is the rational aspect of your mental state that constantly processes the things you think and talk about. This level of consciousness includes your memories, although not present in the conscious mind but can be recalled and retrieved easily into your conscious state and awareness.

The unconscious mind: Your unconscious mind is a tank of memories, thoughts, aspirations, feelings, and urges that are not part of our conscious awareness. The unconscious mind can hold unpleasant feelings and emotions such as pain, conflict, resentment, or anxiety.

Psychoanalytic psychologists believe that psychological problems are entrenched in our unconscious minds. Therefore, the visible symptoms result from unpleasant emotions and feelings hidden in the subconscious.

How Psychoanalytic Treatment Works

Psychoanalytic treatment centers on drawing out the repressed feelings, emotions, and experiences to the conscious, where the patient can face them and deal with them.

Freud believed that by making the unconscious conscious, people could gain insights into their inner conflicts and be cured. People can be helped and cured after experiencing a cleansing of their conflicting unconscious.

The core concept of CBT is rooted in the understanding that feelings, thoughts, and actions are all linked together. Therefore, CBT treatments include changing how we think to make lasting and positive changes in how we feel. Awareness of our thought patterns enables us to recognize unhealthy and dysfunctional thoughts, empowering us to create new ones and act differently. Meanwhile, psychoanalysis helps us achieve this by bringing the unconscious to the conscious awareness for us to deal with.

Note: It is important to keep in mind that while you seek a therapist who you'd feel comfortable with to begin your healing and self-awareness journey, you need to be responsible for your thoughts, feelings, and actions, even when you've started your treatment. Your therapist can only guide you through your thoughts, not be responsible for your choices, actions, or decisions.

Your therapist will be there to help you clarify your challenging thoughts and point you toward dealing with certain emotions or situations. You may find it difficult, disturbing, and even painful at the beginning, but it will improve as you attain a new level of understanding of how your mind works and how to control your actions better.

Life will definitely get easier as you develop this mental resilience.

What if you need to set boundaries without cutting family ties?

Below are tips to help you set boundaries with family members without cutting off ties in conflicted relationships and a powerful exercise to help you deal with your resentments.

Understanding the behavior of a toxic person

Understanding the behavior of a toxic person can help you set the right boundaries. For example, this person could be nice in other areas and probably have a genuine love for you. However, you don't seem happy keeping a good relationship with them. If you still feel negative emotions from this person, it could mean they hurt with some of their actions, or you've been deeply hurt in the past and find it difficult to move on. In this case, by understanding their behavior, you might decide to put some space between you by taking some time off to reflect and focus on yourself.

Observing patterns and behavior

By observing the patterns and behaviors of the present unhealthy relationship, no matter what they've done, you will see clearly if you would be better off without the person in your life or not. By observing their patterns, you understand that you don't need to make excuses for them or try to rationalize their behaviors toward you when you. For example, *"He hit me because I accused him while he was having a bad day. I guess it was my fault."*

Recap of the 7 Survival Secrets given in this book

1 - Understanding the behavior of a toxic person.

2 - Observe and reflect on your family patterns and traditions.

3 - How to mindfully set boundaries and understand what causes you painful emotions - 5 Weeks Exercise in Chapter 3.

4 - Make a decision to deal with it: stay with them, or go away for an undetermined time to facilitate healing.

5 - Understanding your traumas, letting go of self-sabotage, shame, guilt, and fear.

6 - Keep a room for better days. Maintain contact from time to time for new opportunities for healing.

7 - Encouraging yourself to seek support in therapy, understanding the benefits of an effective and professional company to talk through your issues and reach a higher self.

Exercise for Resentment

Are you ready to deal with your resentment? Then let's get started.

- It would help if you found a quiet place where you won't be interrupted
- Choose a comfortable position; it could be either sitting or lying down.
- Close your eyes, relax your body and breathe slowly

- Now, imagine yourself in a theater where everywhere is dark except the small stage in front of you
- Allow the person you resent to climb onto the stage (this person can be alive or dead or in the present or the past)
- Visualize good things happening to the person. Select the things the person would find meaningful, love, and appreciate. Let them experience and enjoy those things
- Imagine them being happy and satisfied. Visualize them smiling and filled with happiness.
- Sustain this image for a few minutes, then engrave it into your mind as a memory of a past event that happened
- Now, let the person leave the stage
- Next, it's your turn to take the stage
- This time, you'll visualize good things you'll appreciate and find useful happening to you. Let the image be as vividly as possible
- See yourself smiling and happy.

- After a few minutes, engrave it as a memory, then exit your mental space.
- Make this into a daily exercise and continue for 20 days. You'll see your resentments fading away since you no longer hate the person. Instead, positive feelings and thoughts will replace negative feelings.

The power of this technique lies in how you engage in this exercise. This technique becomes more powerful the more you repeat it, and you will begin to feel the effects over time. Remember to do this exercise where you won't be disturbed. I suggest you get a note and write down your progress by documenting any changes you experience.

198 customer reviews

⭐⭐⭐⭐⭐ 5.0 out of 5 stars ⌄

5 star	████████████	99%
4 star		0%
3 star		0%
2 star		1%
1 star		0%

Review this product

Share your thoughts with other customers

Write a customer review

Review

If you've found this book helpful so far, kindly leave me with a 5-star review on Amazon! This will help this book reach more and more people, increasing the chances for a better mentality and mental health in companies worldwide!

We haven't finished our journey yet, but your review would mean the world to me, as we could reach more readers craving tools to cope with similar situations!

Conclusion

Well Done!

I commend you for staying with me until this milestone of the book. Dealing with toxic relatives can be difficult and quite challenging. I know this because I've experienced it. Toxic relatives can leave you feeling empty and broken, making you question your sanity and identity.

No one deserves to experience traumatic situations, but sadly it happens, and we use it to evolve in this life. It is even more difficult to handle when the toxicity comes from the closest people. You are supposed to trust and rely on these people to love you unconditionally.

I know it must have been heart-breaking to endure what could be described as one of the most challenging periods of your life. However, I hope this book shines a light on your situation by equipping you with the right tools to regain control of your life. You need to take full control and be responsible for your life. Rediscover and redefine yourself, and let your actions result from the decisions you've made.

Remember the popular saying, *"practice leads to perfection."* With this in mind, let's do a quick recap of what we've discussed so far. These will be the key points to remember as you fight back to free yourself from toxicity and create the best future for you.

We started by discussing what an abusive relationship is, who is a toxic person, and the realization that anyone could be toxic towards you, including your loved ones. We also discussed the need to acknowledge toxic behaviors by understanding abusive people's patterns and what you should be on the lookout for. We also emphasized self-control and how to react to patronizing behaviors.

Achieving the first steps will lay the foundation you need to take the other steps necessary to free yourself from toxic relatives.

I am confident you've learned invaluable skills that should help you deal with the toxic people in your life.

So far, we have covered together, and you've:

- ○ Realized that you need to forgive and accept yourself.
- ○ Understood your emotions, learnt more about yourself, and found ways to respond to abusive situations.
- ○ Learned to make your own decisions and how your choices will affect your future.
- ○ Learned more about self-destruction, self-sabotage, and possible reasons why people self-sabotage. Also, don't forget that you need to let go of shame, guilt, fear, and all negative emotions you might have consciously or unconsciously developed.
- ○ Discovered what psychotherapy is and how it can help you. This resource isn't as scary or intimidating as you might have conjured or imagined it to be.

- You've been fully equipped with the knowledge to help you heal and redefine your life and purpose.

It's been a great experience knowing that we embarked on this journey together and finally reached this point. I want to leave you with positive lines that helped me during my early days battling toxic relationships.

Affirm to yourself:

- **I can create a better life!**
- **I won't give up on the hard work I've put into my recovery.**
- **I will always pick myself up and keep moving even when I fall.**

You may think that it is impossible to take these actions within your environment. But you can definitely do it, and you can be the change. Start creating the life you want for yourself before your surroundings create that for you. Please don't stop fighting to get a life free from toxicity and negativity because you deserve it, and you can definitely cope with it healthily.

If you've found this book helpful to you in any way and it has inspired or impacted your life towards recovery, kindly leave me with a 5-star review; this will help this content to be pushed forward and reach more people.

I wish you the best choices and mindfulness as you start a new journey in your life!

A Free 4 Steps Guide To Understand Your Emotional Patterns is yours now!

This is a special gift for you, as you are consuming one of our books! This **4 Steps Guide** will take you through the possible patterns you have and ways to reframe them + Exercises!

Access

www.mindfulpersona.com

to get your free copy today!

Resources

Champion, L. (2019, June 17). 9 *Signs You Were Raised in a Toxic Family (and How to Move On)*. PureWow.

https://www.purewow.com/wellness/toxic-family-signs

Williamson, J. (2017, July 20). *11 Ways to Keep Your Peace in a Toxic Environment*. Healing Brave.

https://healingbrave.com/blogs/all/how-to-keep-your-peace-toxic-environment

Gervais, S.J., Vescio, T.K. The Effect of Patronizing Behavior and Control on Men and Women's Performance in Stereotypically Masculine Domains. Sex Roles 66, 479–491 (2012).

https://doi-org.proxy.lib.sfu.ca/10.1007/s11199-011-0115-1

Su, Amy Jen, and Muriel Maignan Wilkins. "Which Behaviors Must Leaders Avoid?" Harvard Business Review, 14 Dec. 2013,

https://hbr.org/2013/05/which-behaviors-do-leaders-mos

Goldstein, E. (2021, April 19). *4 Reasons You're Repeating Unhealthy Family Patterns & What You Can Do About It — Integrative Psychotherapy Mental Health Blog*. Integrative Psychotherapy & Trauma Treatment.

https://integrativepsych.co/new-blog/heal-family-dysfunction-long-island

Ackerman, C. E., MA. (2022, May 25). *13 Emotional Intelligence Activities & Exercises*. PositivePsychology.Com.

https://positivepsychology.com/emotional-intelligence-exercises/

Van Dyke, K. (2021, August 20). *When Letting Go Is Tough: How to Emotionally Detach from Someone*. Psych Central.

https://psychcentral.com/lib/the-what-why-when-and-how-of-detaching-from-loved-ones

Wilson, C. R., PhD. (2022, May 23). *What Is Self-Sabotage? How to Help Stop the Vicious Cycle*. PositivePsychology.Com.

https://positivepsychology.com/self-sabotage/

Why Empathy Is Important. (2020, May 2). Verywell Mind.

https://www.verywellmind.com/what-is-empathy-2795562

K. Soriano, C. G. (2022, April 25). PSYCOM.

https://www.psycom.net/personality-disorders/narcissistic/

Raypole, C. (2022, May 17). *Cognitive Behavioral Therapy: What Is It and How Does It Work?* Healthline.

https://www.healthline.com/health/cognitive-behavioral-thera py#What-is-cognitive-behavioral-therapy

GoodTherapy Editor Team. (2017, November 27). *Psychoanalysis / Modern Psychoanalysis.* GT.

https://www.goodtherapy.org/learn-about-therapy/types/psych oanalysis

Milton Keynes UK
Ingram Content Group UK Ltd.
UKHW040112090224
437448UK00001B/166